ALLEYN'S

The Coeducational School

GOD'S GIFT

Alleyn's School Main Building   *(Rutherford)*

ALLEYN'S
The Coeducational School

ARTHUR R CHANDLER

Gresham Books Limited
in partnership with
Alleyn's School

© Arthur R Chandler

First published in 1998
by
Gresham Books Ltd
Henley on Thames, Oxfordshire, England

in partnership with
Alleyn's School
Dulwich, London

ISBN 0946 095 337

Design and typesetting by The Heritage Consultancy
Printed and bound in Great Britain by
M P G Books, Bodmin

Dedicated, with his knowledge and permission, to

DEREK A. FENNER
Headmaster 1976–1992

The Author's thanks are recorded

to Dr Colin Niven for his enthusiasm and support

to those who have loaned photographs

to Peter Rodway, AOB, for his assistance in general research especially in the compilation of the various lists

to Lt Col E M D Jones for information on the Combined Cadet Force

to Peter Reeve, AOB, for information from his personal records

to Caroline Sherlock for assistance in selection of photographs

to Jennifer Ferguson for technical assistance

to Valerie Chandler for the index

to Patrick Darby, OA for the use of the Dulwich Map of 1626

Unless otherwise stated the photographs used in this book
are from the School Archive
or from the Personal Archive of the author

All royalties are being donated to the School

CONTENTS

Edward Alleyn
1566–1626
Founder of The College of God's Gift
1619

THE MANOR OF DULWICH

OVER the last thousand years more than thirty different spellings have been given to the area we now know as Dulwich. Its earliest recorded spelling is in the *Codex Diplomaticus* where we are told that in 967 A.D. a portion of ground known as 'Dilwihs' was granted by King Eadgar to one of his thanes. All spellings of the place-name have been derived from the Anglo-Saxon 'Dael' meaning Valley and 'Wic' meaning Village. The Village in the Valley of the tenth century has become the Dulwich of today.

During the next century the property must have reverted to Royal owner-ship for we find, ninety-nine years later, that it belonged to the Saxon King Harold who was killed at the Battle of Hastings. After the Conquest all lands were seized by William of Normandy and were held by the Crown. In 1082 Aylwin Child built a Priory on Crown land situated on the bank of the River Thames on the northern edge of the Manor of Bermondsey. William Rufus presented the complete Manor to the Bermondsey Priory in 1094. Thirty-three years later, Henry I granted the Manor of Dulwich to Bermondsey Priory thus creating a link that was to remain until the Reformation.

Dulwich Manor was used by the Priory both as a source of income, from various rents, and also as a garden from which many of the day-to-day needs of the monastic establishment were supplied. Originally the Priory was controlled by nominees from France but the Anglicised monks became dissatisfied with this situation especially when it was realised that a large amount of the Priory's income was leaving the English Kingdom for foreign shores.

Towards the end of the fourteenth century the monastery was made independent of foreign control and Richard Denton was appointed and installed as the first English Prior. Eventually, in 1399, the Priory was raised to the status of an Abbey.

Robert Wharton was the last Abbot of Bermondsey and he was forced to surrender the Abbey and all its possessions, including the Manor of Dulwich, to the King's Men on 1st January, 1538. The Manor again reverted to the Crown.

Henry VIII wanted money so he sold his newly acquired lands to loyal supporters. On 11th October, 1544, Thomas Calton, a Goldsmith of the City of London, purchased the Manor of Dulwich from the Crown for six hundred and nine pounds, eighteen shillings and two pence. In the previous month Thomas had bought Rigate's Green (in Dulwich Woods) from Sir Humphrey Browne. This was incorporated into the Manor and when Thomas Calton died the whole estate descended to his son Nicholas. Nicholas died in 1575, when his son Francis was only ten years old. The property was well looked after on the minor's behalf and Francis received the livery of his inheritance in the year 1587. He was probably knighted in that or the following year. The Manor prospered under the guidance of Sir Francis but, after eighteen years, he decided the time had come to sell his estate. In 1605 he sold the Manor of Dulwich to Edward Alleyn.

The Fortune Theatre (Reconstruction)

EDWARD ALLEYN

ON 2nd SEPTEMBER, 1566, three children were baptised at the Church of Saint Botolph, Bishopsgate: Edward Alleyn, Henry Wood and Olive Clerk. Our interest lies in the first of these whose grandfather was Thomas Alleyn of Willen, in Buckinghamshire, and of Mesham, in Bedfordshire. The second son of this gentleman was called Edward and he had become Innkeeper of 'The Pye' at Bishopsgate in London. Edward had married Margaret, the daughter of John Townley of Towneley, in Lancashire, and their son, Edward Junior, was naturally baptised in the church within whose parish the Pye Inn was situated.

The Innkeeper died while his son was still a child and his widow Margaret married an actor called Brown whose influence on his stepson, young Edward, was to have a lasting effect upon the Elizabethan/Jacobean theatre and, in time, upon the Manor of Dulwich.

There being no actresses at this time, it can be assumed that Edward Alleyn played female parts during his boyhood as was then the custom. At the age of eighteen his name was recorded in the list of the Earl of Worcester's Players. At this time Bankside, Southwark, was fast becoming a gathering ground for the entertainments of the City of London and it was here that Alleyn met Philip Henslowe, a shrewd businessman and entrepreneur with great interests in theatres, sideshows and the like. Alleyn soon became a business partner of Henslowe and on 22nd October, 1592, he married Henslowe's stepdaughter, Joan Woodwarde. The newly married couple took up residence on Bankside in the Liberty of the Clink, within the Parish of Saint Saviour.

At the end of the sixteenth century Edward Alleyn was acclaimed as the leading actor of the time. He led, with Henslowe, the company of Players known as 'My Lord Admiral's Men', later to become 'The Prince's Men' in the reign of James I & VI. He took the leading roles in the four great plays of Christopher Marlowe, *Edward II*, *Tamburlaine*, *The Jew of Malta* and *Dr. Faustus*. All of these were written before Marlowe's thirtieth birthday. It is believed that, while at Cambridge, Marlowe had been recruited for government work, probably as a spy. This activity was later to lead to the great playwright's early demise in May 1593 when he was stabbed to death in a tavern at Deptford.

Marlowe's death did not seem to have an effect on Alleyn's good fortune. In the same year there was a visitation of the plague to London and the actors of the main companies became strolling players throughout the land in order to escape infection and, in so doing, bring themselves to new audiences and new sources of income . The ladies, however, obviously felt themselves quite safe on Bankside as Mrs Alleyn and Mrs Henslowe both remained at home! Eventually the plague left London and the actors returned to the Liberty of the Clink where Alleyn and Henslowe continued their various profitable enterprises.

The Bear Pit flourished and the Rose Theatre was extremely successful. Alongside these two Alleyn/Henslowe ventures on Bankside were those of 'My Lord Chamberlain's Men' headed by William Shakespeare and James Burbage.

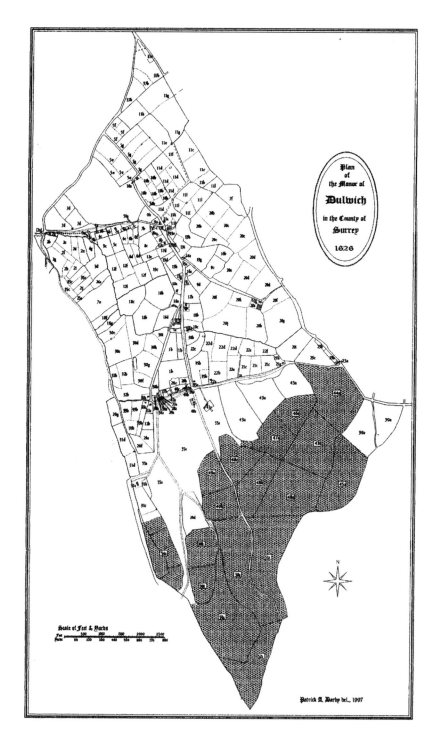

The Manor of Dulwich, 1626   *Darby*

With a performance of *Hamlet* in January 1601 Shakespeare opened the Globe Theatre on Bankside having brought across the Thames the original timbers of 'The Theatre' in Shoreditch. Not to be outdone, Alleyn built the Fortune Theatre in the Parish of Saint Giles, Cripplegate, and opened it in May of the same year. The new theatre was "like the late erected Plaiehouse on the Banck in the saide Parishe of Ste Saviours called the Globe". Although Alleyn retired from acting in the following year, he remained manager of the Fortune Theatre until it was destroyed by fire on 9th December 1621.

Bear-baiting was a substantial source of income to Alleyn who was appointed by James I &VI to be his 'Chief Master, Ruler and Overseer of all and singular of his majestie's games, of bears, and bulls, and mastive dogs, and mastive bitches'. This authorised him to take any bulls, bears or dogs from any part of the kingdom for the service of the king on payment of a 'fair price'. Dogs were taken by Alleyn from the Bear Garden to the Tower of London in order to bait a lion in his den. In the early seventeenth century the Court gained much pleasure from animal baiting and this must have necessitated a great deal of forward planning for the 'Chief Master'. His acting talents, however, were not completely lost after his retirement from the stage, as Alleyn delivered congratulatory addresses on special occasions such as the City Pageant staged in March 1603 in honour of the Sovereign's visit.

In 1605 Edward Alleyn began negotiations with Sir Francis Calton for the purchase of the Manor of Dulwich and in October of the following year was styled 'Lord of the Manor of Dulwich'. Having attained this position at the age of forty he must have considered his next moves carefully. One legend records that some years previously he had been acting on stage where there were a number of attendant devils but, on counting them, he found there was one too many and realised that the real devil had appeared to him. He thereupon vowed to build a charitable institution to atone for any irregularities in his methods of earning an income. This cannot be substantiated but we do know that he showed an interest in the Charterhouse Foundation created in 1611 and visited it more than once. At the same time Edward Wilson, Vicar of Camberwell, founded a Grammar School which was to carry his name. In 1610 Alleyn became Warden of the Liberty of the Clink and set about plans for his own charitable foundation. All records show him to be a worthy man and it was his personal belief that his gift of acting and his ability in business ventures were gifts to him from Above. The title he bestowed on his Foundation reflects this in his choice of name for ALLEYN'S COLLEGE OF GOD'S GIFT.

The original constitution of his College provided for a Master and a Warden (both of whom should have the name of Alleyn), four Fellows - preacher, usher, schoolmaster and organist, six poor brethren, six poor sisters and twelve poor scholars. The brethren and the sisters would live in almshouses which were to be built as an integral part of the College.

Alleyn gave instructions for his College to be erected at the south end of the main street of the Hamlet of Dulwich. Work started in 1613 and took three years to complete. This building consisted of a centre block containing a Chapel and the residences for the Master, Warden and Fellows. The West Wing

George Abbot, Archbishop of Caterbury   *(Guildford Library)*

contained the accommodation of the twelve poor scholars and the East Wing was for the twelve almspeople. The Chapel, and the burial ground at the north end of the Village, were consecrated on 1st September, 1616, by George Abbot Archbishop of Canterbury, during a vacancy in the See of Winchester. Some poor brethren were admitted in the same year but it was not until 21st June, 1619, that Letters Patent were issued under the Great Seal of James I & VI allowing Alleyn to establish a College in Dulwich. On the following 13th September a great banquet was held and Alleyn recorded in his diary "This day was ye foundacon of ye Colledge finisht".

After thirty-one years of happily married life, Joan Alleyn died on 28th June, 1623. All records show a complete partnership and constancy between the two and yet, on 3rd December in the same year, Alleyn married the nineteen-year-old Constance, daughter of The Revd Dr John Donne, Dean of St Paul's and Lord of the Manor of neighbouring Nunhead. The marriage took place at the Parish Church of St Giles, Camberwell.

Three years later Edward Alleyn died and was buried in the Chapel of his College on 27th November, 1626. He had no children - his descendants and beneficiaries are the scholars and pupils of the Foundation and the inhabitants of Dulwich.

Bankside, Southwark

Canon Carver

THE COLLEGE OF GOD'S GIFT

FOR THE ORIGINAL College of God's Gift, the six poor brethren, six poor sisters and the twelve poor scholars had to be chosen from the four parishes with which Alleyn had been connected: Saint Giles, Camberwell (in which Dulwich was situated), Saint Saviour, Southwark (where the Bear Pit stood on Bankside), Saint Botolph, Bishopsgate (where Alleyn was born) and Saint Giles Cripplegate (where stood the Fortune Theatre). It was also laid down that both Master and Warden should have the surname of Alleyn and that both should be unmarried. In fact the first holders of these Offices were both married and had been appointed by the Founder himself. Thomas Alleyn, a cousin of Edward and a barber-surgeon of the City of London, was appointed Master on 13th September, 1619, but did not actually assume office until the death of the Founder in November 1626. Thomas Alleyn had a son and two daughters. He died in March 1631. Mathias Alleyn, also a cousin of Edward, was appointed Warden on 13th September, 1619, but also did not assume office until November 1626. He succeeded as Master in 1631. His son, John, was elected Warden in 1669 and succeeded as Master in January 1677-8. He also was married - the 'unmarried' rule was never strictly observed and the 'surname' rule was to cause great difficulties for the Foundation for the next two centuries.

Since the consecration of the Chapel by Archbishop George Abbot, Archbishops of Canterbury have held the title of Visitor. The title is now an honorary one but the second Visitor, Archbishop Laud, found he had to take specific action to save and solidify the Foundation. The original building was not well constructed and soon needed repairs. As early as 1638 the Corporation was dissolved by Archbishop Laud for six months during which time the building was repaired and general affairs were straightened out to enable the Foundation to continue its work for the scholars and almspeople. It was not easy for the Foundation to run smoothly - the four parishes, as beneficiaries, were always claiming 'rights' from the Foundation estates and the Masters, generally, seemed very unsuitable people to have in control of the College.

There was one notable exception, James Allen, who added a 'y' as the penultimate letter of his name before applying for the post of Warden to which he was elected in May, 1712. On later being promoted to Master on 1st September 1721 he dropped the 'y' after which all Masters had the surname Allen until 1858. James Allen gave six houses near the Kensington gravel pits to the Foundation in 1741 stipulating that the rents from these properties should provide for a free school for the teaching of poor boys and girls in Dulwich. This school became James Allen's Girls' School by Act of Parliament just over a century later.

At other times applicants for the post of Master were not nearly so interested in education. The applicants to succeed James Allen included a vintner, a Paul's schoolmaster, a hosier, a peruke maker, a linen draper and a malt factor. The successful applicant was Joseph Allen, the malt factor!

One other 'good' appointment was made - that of John Allen as Warden in 1811. He became Master nine years later and served as such for twenty-three years. John Allen was a writer of distinction. His works included *An enquiry into the rise and growth of the Royal Prerogative in England* and 'The Life of Fox' for the seventh and eighth editions of the *Encyclopaedia Britannica*. He was looked upon as a very able and well informed man. It was during his Mastership that a 'New Grammar School' was built near the Foundation buildings and opened in 1842.

In 1857 the old Corporation was dissolved by Act of Parliament and the Alleyn Foundation was reconstituted as two sections - Educational and Eleemosynary. Two Schools were created, the Upper School, which was to be housed 'in the Old College or in a new building', and the Lower School, mainly for the 'poor scholars', which was to be housed in 'suitable buildings'. The Master, George Allen, the Warden, Richard Allen and the four Fellows were all pensioned off on the 31st December that year.

The same Act of Parliament permitted an appointment to the Mastership without restriction to surname and The Revd Canon James Carver was appointed Master in 1858. In 1870 the Upper School moved to a new building on Dulwich Common whilst the Lower School was taught in the School Wing of the original building and the Grammar School nearby.

During the Mastership of Canon Carver the residential area within the Alleyn Estate expanded considerably and the income to the Foundation increased likewise. Even so the Charity Commissioners seemed to be only inter-ested in the Upper School of Alleyn's College of God's Gift and in 1876 declared that the Lower School should be closed. The College Governors did not object and were willing to allow such a closure to take place. However, the Master of the College did object and made his voice heard in many quarters. At his own expense Canon Carver appealed to the Judicial Committee of the Privy Council. He won the day and the closure scheme was withdrawn by the Commissioners. Eventually a new scheme was submitted expressly retaining the Lower School and giving it the name 'Alleyn's School'.

On 18th August, 1882, the Royal Assent was given to the plan for the reorganisation of the Alleyn Foundation, and Alleyn's School became an educa-tional establishment in its own right although it was to share the same Board of Governors as Dulwich College for well into the next century. Canon Carver retained the Mastership of Dulwich College for one year and then received a pension. The Master of the Lower College, The Revd Joseph Henry Smith, became the first Headmaster of Alleyn's School.

First Crest of Alleyn's School

The Old College, Dulwich Village

The Revd J.H. Smith

THE REVD J. H. SMITH, 1882–1902

WHEN The Revd Joseph Henry Smith was appointed Headmaster of Alleyn's School in 1882 he well knew the staff, pupils and even the building over which he was to rule, for he had been 'The Master' of the Lower School of Alleyn's College of God's Gift since 1875. It was this Lower School that was to become Alleyn's School and it was the pupils from this Lower School who were to form the Edward Alleyn Club. There were two 'Masters' of the Lower School before Smith: they were Dr W.F. Greenfield (1858-1870) and the Revd B.C. Huntley (1870-1875).

There is in existence *A Dictionary of the English Language* that contains the following inscription "W.E. Groom. 1871. Used by me when at School at Dulwich during Dr Greenfield & Revd B.C. Huntley's Headmasterships". Young Groom was twelve years old when he wrote this. One hundred and eleven years later his two sons, Victor and Reginald, both AOBs and both in their eighties, were present at the planting ceremony of the Centenary Tree on Founder's Day, 1982.

In 1858 the Lower School had started with thirty-three boys, including 'the twelve poor scholars'. By the late 1870s this number had risen to one hundred and sixty and in 1882 was two hundred and twenty-five. Of these we can see twelve in the photograph of the last Foundation Scholars (see page 22) and we can read the words of another. This boy was George Swift who was at the School from 1879 to 1886 and who, during the 1940's, told the author of this present history about schooldays in the Village.

In 1949 G.E.J. Swift wrote: "It may be remembered ... The Upper School met in the buildings on the west side of the Quad [today the green before the Chapel] the Lower School in the one-room building on the corner of Gallery Road. In 1870, when the Upper School moved to the New College [Dulwich College], the Lower School took over its quarters. There I spent my schooldays. The Revd. J.H. Smith was headmaster. The masters included Messrs Jenkins, Marsland, Kinsey, W.R. Carter, Nightingale, Dennis, Brabham, M. Petré; also Roper and Brading, later to found houses".

"Our school hours were 9-1 and 1.30 - 3.30, except Tuesday and Thursday when we had half-an-hour's drill. We paraded in the Quad for dismissal each afternoon unless very wet. The Drum and Fife Band played for about ten minutes and the headmaster took the salute."

George Swift related the story that prior to 1882, Canon Carver had walked down from the "new" College each Friday afternoon in order to administer the corporal punishment "earned" during the week. He also recalled a French master who held boys out of the first floor windows in what are now the Estates Offices in order to encourage pupils to learn their French verbs! Such were the days.

The Last Foundation Scholars, 1883

The differences between the summer and autumn terms of 1882 might not have seemed very great to young Swift and his companions save that Canon Carver no longer "walked down the road". The Scheme of 1882 had laid in specific terms regulations to enable Alleyn's to become an educational establishment in its own right. Clauses in the Scheme included:

"The Upper School of the College of God's Gift shall, except where herein expressed, be named Dulwich College, and what is meant by the term Dulwich College as used in this scheme. The Lower School of the College of God's Gift shall, except where otherwise herein expressed, be named Alleyn's School.

". . . [the Estates Governors] shall, from and after the opening of the new buildings for Alleyn's School, pay to the College Governors for the purposes of such School the annual sum of one thousand pounds, to be carried by them to the credit of Alleyn's School Account, and be treated as income."

Dulwich College was given four thousand pounds annually to be treated as income and was open to any boy between the ages of ten and nineteen years with the requisite academic qualifications, but as far as Alleyn's was concerned, Clause 100 of the Scheme stated:

"No boy shall be admitted into the School under the age of eight years. No boy shall remain in the School after the age of sixteen years, or, if he attains that age during a School term, then after the end of such term, except with the permission of the College Governors, which in special cases may be given upon the recommendation of the Head Master."

It should be noted that until July 1995 Dulwich College and Alleyn's School shared the same Board of Governors. The clauses set down in the Scheme must soon have had an impact on the pupils. Pupils at the School were trained for trade or commerce and subjects taught were mainly English and Mathematics, French and Elementary Science. The low compulsory leaving age restricted boys from reaching higher academic attainment although scholarships were offered for boys to complete their education at Dulwich College. Even so, results in the Cambridge Local Examinations were good. In 1885 the School headed the pass list in Natural Science and the following year it was an Alleyn's boy who was first in Botany.

Twelve thousand pounds were allocated for the building of a new Alleyn's School and a portion of ground was set aside for this purpose a quarter of a mile to the north-east of the Village. Townley Road was specially made in order to give ample access from Lordship Lane and the single School building costing thirteen thousand, eight hundred and five pounds was surrounded by thirteen acres of playing fields. In October 1887 the new School was ready. The Headmaster assembled the School, now 250 strong, in the Old Quad for the last time and then, headed by the School band, Alleyn's marched through the Village and across the fields to Townley Road where Joseph Henry Smith "took possession" of the new establishment.

The School contained sixteen "commodius" classrooms, offices, kitchens, and servants' quarters but it had "no gym and the field was a wilderness where the pheasant waged incessant war on the mangel-wurzle".

New Science Building (now in CDT Block)

In the Village, 1883

At the New School, 1887

Smith's Walk

Made wide enough to take a horse and cart, a path was cut from the Village to Alleyn's to enable easy access. This path was called "Smith's Walk". Boys walked to the School, which was to serve the local community extremely well.

With the move in 1887 Latin and German were added to the curriculum and Smith set about demanding a high standard of academic work from all. Just before leaving the Old College, Alleyn's School played the last official game of rugger in its history. It won this game which, incidentally, was against Dulwich College! Smith decided, against a good deal of opposition, that soccer was to be the sport for his new School - rugger was banned. He did this with the expressed intention of widening the differences between the two Foundation Schools. Cricket was played with distinction when, in 1890, Bradley, the School Cricket Captain, took ninety wickets for 360 runs for the School 1st XI (still a record). He later played for Kent, the Gentlemen and for England against Australia in the fourth and fifth tests.

The second building to be erected in the grounds was the porter's lodge to be followed in 1894 by a science and woodwork block. The buttery was in the basement of the main School and the layout of the fields improved every year with the Headmaster personally selecting sites for the trees and shrubs that were to be put around the School's boundaries and within the grounds. The Headmaster's lawn appeared and on it stood the school band each afternoon to play "The Fusiliers" while the school marched past as a dismissal ceremony, doffing their caps to the Headmaster who stood on the steps.

In November 1890 the first number of the *Edward Alleyn Magazine* was published. In this was recorded both news of Old Boys' activities and reports on the School and its staff. Ten years later Smith quarrelled with the Old Boys as he insisted on the right of censoring this publication. At the Old Boys Dinner in 1900 there was nobody present to reply to the Toast "The School and masters" - the Headmaster had forbidden his staff to attend!

In October 1901, the School produced its own *Alleyn's School Magazine*, the first sentence being "With the Head Master's sanction, and in response to general desire, it has been decided that the school shall enjoy a magazine of its own". Two magazines were therefore published each term (one by the School, one by the Edward Alleyn Club) until they were amalgamated in March, 1904.

When Smith retired in 1902 the School had nearly 700 boys. He had had a long and dominating influence upon the creation of Alleyn's - for twenty-seven years he had been at the helm. That his closing years were marked by a disagreement between himself and the Old Boys Club was a great source of regret to his former pupils and they joined the staff and pupils in a testimonial, taking the form of a portrait to be hung in the Great hall, with a personal present of a silver dessert service together with a bromide reproduction of the painting.

F H Kirby, VC   *Royal Engineers Museum*

GROUP CAPTAIN F. H. KIRBY, VC, CBE, DCM

Frank Howard Kirby was one of the first pupils of the newly designated Alleyn's School in 1882. Like many boys at that period he left after only two years. In his case, however, his parents moved away from Dulwich.

In 1892 he enlisted in the Royal Engineers and was sent to South Africa with his Regiment at the start of the Boer War in 1899. He was awarded the Victoria Cross for gallantry on 2nd June 1900.

The citation from *The London Gazette* of 5th October 1900 reads

"Corporal Frank Howard Kirby, Royal Engineers

"On the morning of 2nd June 1900, a party sent to try to cut the Delago Bay Railway were retiring, hotly pressed by very superior numbers.

"During one of the successive retirements of the rear-guard, a man whose horse had been shot was seen running after his comrades. He was a long way behind the rest of his troop and was under brisk fire.

"From amongst the retiring troop, Corporal Kirby turned and rode back to the man's assistance. Although by the time he reached him they were under heavy fire at close range, Corporal Kirby managed to get the dismounted man up behind him and take him clear over the next rise held by our rearguard. This is the third occasion on which Corporal Kirby has displayed gallantry in the face of the enemy."

The Victoria Cross is the highest British decoration for 'conspicuous bravery or devotion to the country in the presence of the enemy'. The scroll on the bronze cross is superscribed 'For Valour'.

Frank Kirby became the Regimental Sergeant Major at the Royal Engineers Depot at Chatham from 1906 until 1911. He was commissioned into the Royal Flying Corps in 1912 and was on active service during the Great War.

In 1922 he returned to the School as Colonel Kirby, a most honoured Old Boy, to unveil the War Memorial in the Great Hall. The title of the Royal Flying Corps was changed to the Royal Air Force from which he retired in the rank of Group Captain.

He died on 8th July 1956.

Frank Kirby's portrait hangs in the entrance hall of the School
with a miniature sculpture of his heroic exploit nearby

H.B. Baker and Staff

H. B. BAKER, 1902–1903

AFTER the Whitsun Holidays, 1902, the new Headmaster arrived in the person of H.B. Baker, MA, FRS, who had been for many years a Science Master at Dulwich College. One of his first duties was to announce the end of the Boer War and to inform the boys that the Boers had now enrolled under the British Flag and were part of the British Empire.

He had been a member of the Council of the Chemical Society of London since 1899 and had many chemical discoveries attributed to him. At the College he had been an excellent disciplinarian and the Governors thought fit to appoint a leading scientist as the Headmaster in order to remodel the school for the 'modern' world.

He divided the School above the Lower Fourth into Modern and Science Sides, the former concentrating on French and German with the addition of book-keeping and shorthand whilst the latter was to make ample provision for boys who would follow a calling where a scientific training would be of the most value to them, whether as electrical engineers, manufacturing chemists, or possibly as inventors. In order to ensure success the number in each form was limited to thirty.

His three ideals were honesty, manners and work. He told the boys that those who talked about nothing but games were wrong. They should play heartily while at their games but, once these were finished, they should devote their whole attention to their work. He instituted a system of prefects and made great educational changes which were to put the school on the public school level. However, his love of Chemistry was such that he left after only one year for a post at Oxford.

School Report, 1902

31

F. Collins and Staff, 1911

F. COLLINS, 1903–1920

F. COLLINS arrived as Headmaster at the start of Advent Term 1903. He had previously been Headmaster of the Central Foundation School and was to guide Alleyn's into a programme befitting the start of the Twentieth Century.

When on 21st March, 1904, the Memorial Tablet to those who served and those who died in the South African War was unveiled by Mr Baker, the previous Headmaster, Mr Collins could not have realised that his tenure of office would include a much heavier sacrifice of the School's sons. Five Old Boys had been killed and over fifty others, including a VC, had served in the Boer War. It is interesting to note that the cost of the Memorial was £31.7s.0d. It is now situated over the doorway that leads to the corridor at the rear of the Great Hall.

On 16th March, 1904, the Old Boys' and School magazines were amalgamated under one banner and both past and present pupils could read of each other's activities once more. The Sixth Form social evening was reported in this edition, the entertainment including such items as Mr Brading singing "Nazareth", E. Masters and E. Johnson acting the quarrel scene from "Julius Caesar" and Mr Coates giving an amusing performance of "Rubinstein's Piano Playing". A most enjoyable evening was the verdict!

The Board of Education had inspected the School soon after the arrival of Mr Collins and, from the start of the Academic Year in 1904, the Board had laid down a new set of regulations so that more time would have to be devoted to English and Modern Languages than to Science. In 1905 the Gymnasium was erected and an effort was made to instruct every boy in the use of a rifle. George Swift, already mentioned as a boy in the Village, was now a Lieut.-Colonel and arranged a shooting match between the Old Boys and the School. In the same year A.E. Rawlinson obtained a first class degree in classics at Oxford. He entered the School in 1896, matriculated with honours in January 1901 and became an Exhibitioner to Dulwich College the following term. He left the College, where he was Captain, two years later for Oxford. He entered the Church and later was Bishop of Derby 1936-1959. Like many who had to complete their education at the College during Collins' headmastership, official records show his education as "Dulwich College", forgetting that five of his seven secondary years were spent at Alleyn's.

In the summer of 1907 a new school uniform appeared and was recorded as being a welcome improvement on the variety of garments that had lately been in vogue. At the same time the adoption of the House System was announced. Six Houses were created each to be named for ever after its first Housemaster. In September boys owed their allegiance to a House which was known not only by a name but also by a colour: Mr Brading's was to be Brown, Mr Cribb's to be Mauve, Mr Roper's Yellow, Mr Tulley's Red, Mr Spurgeon's Pink and Mr Brown's Green. An appeal fund was then opened in order to pay for a Pavilion which was started in the summer of 1908 whilst various inter-House sporting activities were taking place for the first time. It was completed in time for the Advent Term and cost £515 of which £250 was paid by the Governors. Inter-house rivalry took root as a way of School life and was

Building the Old Gymnasium, 1905

extended from the playing field to the classroom where points were awarded for academic work.

Attending Service at the Chapel in the Village had been in abeyance for many years, but was resumed in October 1910, when six hundred boys voluntarily attended a service at which the hymns were "The Son of God Goes Forth to War", "Fight the Good Fight" and "Onward Christian Soldiers." The text for the Chaplain's sermon was that used at the Consecration of the Chapel in 1616, "Promise unto your Lord God and keep it". This resumption of worship within the original Foundation building was to herald regular Chapel worship by the School in future years.

For some years Alleyn's had sent a group of boys to the Public Secondary Schools Camp held at Bisley annually for schools without military cadet corps. All boys had to wear the same uniform and be used to military drill as well as being very capable with a rifle. Drill, in fact, formed part of the school curriculum and retired sergeant-majors were often on the staff to give the boys daily drill instruction. The Houses were companies and the House Captains were company commanders. In 1911 there were 23 schools at the Camp. Out of eight competitions, Alleyn's came first in four, second in two and fourth in two.

On Speech Day in July 1914 it was announced that the Estates Governors had given ten acres of additional playing fields on the south side of Townley Road upon which "when funds permitted" they would build a new building to house the Junior School. (The new building was a long time arriving. It came seventy-eight years later on a site north of the School.)

Within a few weeks war had come. A formal application was made to start an Officers' Training Corps but was rejected by the War Office. On 25th September, however, the "Alleyn's Volunteer Training Corps" was started which was affiliated to the Central association of VTCs. Masters, Fathers and boys (over 15 years) all joined and within half a term there were three hundred and sixty in the contingent. Soon thirty had left to join H.M.Forces. Members who had attended at least forty drills were given a special lapel badge. As more went to war, those left were either too old or too young to be allowed by the War Office regulations for such Training units and the Corps was disbanded in February 1915. In the September of that year the Governors approved the formation of a recognised and uniformed Cadet Corps. The Corps had begun. A large number of the Staff already held army commissions. The Captain and Adjutant of the newly formed Corps was C.F. Tyson but he had been in the post for only a few months when he and Captain E.C. Brown went to France. The Commanding Officer, Captain Gregory, carried on but some of his officers and, in turn, all his N.C.Os eventually went on active service. J.E. Appleyard (Brown's), the School Captain at the outbreak of the War, was awarded the Military Cross and killed later in action on 16th April, 1918. Of the fifty-one prefects who went to war nine did not return. Some, the lucky ones, did return to continue their education where they left off. A strange experience for those concerned and stranger still for those of normal school age to have "men" beside them in the classroom.

Alleyn's Volunteer Training Corps 1914

The Headmaster and brother officers (Corps)

During the War there had been no Speech Days. Certificates were given instead of prizes (see photograph on page 39) and Founder's Day was restricted to one or two cricket matches only. The year 1919 marked not only the first "gathering" since the Armistice but also the tercentory of the Foundation. To mark this occasion the School Captain organised an exhibition of relics from the War. All events at this period were aimed at raising money for a War Memorial which had been agreed in principle as early as April 1918. Two hundred and sixty four had given their lives . They were to be remembered by the installation of a School Organ above the platform in the Great Hall. Under the Organ balcony, panels were erected upon which were inscribed the names of the dead.

In July 1915, Cecil L.T.Smith matriculated and left the School for a final year at Dulwich College as his parents were going abroad. In 1917 an Old Boy who had left the School in 1890, E. S. Hornblower, was killed with the Canadian Infantry and therefore his name appeared on the War Memorial. Cecil Smith was present at its unveiling and would have read the name 'Hornblower' on the panels. Smith became a writer under the pseudonym C. S. Forester. Some stories say that he and Hornblower, AOB, were friends - unlikely because of age but an interesting connection.

The War was over. Life would never be the same again. The Junior School had not been built on the new Townley Field. Instead a tin hut had been built by the Chestnut Tree on the Quad as 'temporary' accommodation. In future years it became affectionately known as the 'Tin Tab' and, in fact, lasted nearly half a century. The years had rolled by and the time had come for Mr Collins to retire. Alleyn's House System is his everlasting memorial.

Optical Laboratory, 1899

Cricket: School First Eleven v Masters, 1914

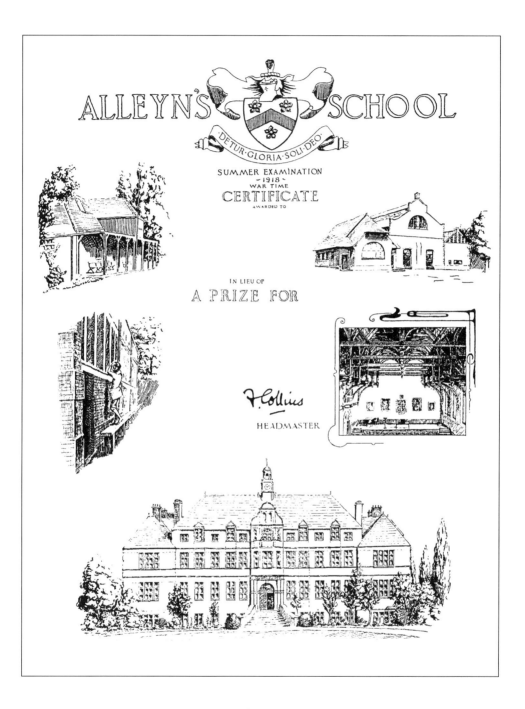

Wartime Certificate in lieu of Prizes

War Memorial   *Ouzman*

THE FOUNDER HOUSEMASTERS

WHEN the House system was inaugurated in 1907 during the Headmastership of F. Collins, six houses were created and it was declared that each was to bear the name of the Founder-Housemaster for evermore. Six colours were chosen for the Houses as follows:

Brading's	Brown	Brown's	Green
Cribb's	Mauve	Roper's	Yellow
Spurgeon's	Pink	Tulley's	Red

It was then thought 'inappropriate' to have blue as a House colour as that was associated in one's mind with the two universities.

Two of these Founders, Roper and Spurgeon, had already left the staff when, in 1921, R B Henderson decided to add two further Houses partly because of their increasing role but mainly to allow for knock-out sports inter-house competitions. Henderson had no qualms about the use of university colours so the two new houses were:

Dutton's	Dark Blue	Tyson's	Light Blue

The eight colours were prominent in the school uniform. The colours were displayed on the back and front section of the school cap and a colour stripe was placed alongside the black and white stripes of the school tie. The quarterings on soccer shirts, the tops of soccer socks and the V line around the cricket sweater clearly showed to which House one belonged.

The Houses have always been strong. Many Old Boys will remember sitting in the Old Buttery at House Tables in strict order of seniority. They will often remember the names of those in their House Team whilst forgetting those in their form. The distinctive colours in the ties and caps brings the House to memory as soon as a person is visualized.

Great pastoral care was shown by the Housemasters and their staff. Discipline that was to the fore on the quad or in the classroom disappeared when the teacher was talking as a Housemaster to a boy as an individual. This kindness is often remembered by many who attended the school.

S. J. BRADING

THE time 'Brad' walked along Townley Road in the mornings never varied by a minute and he always carried with him the smallest leather case that any boy had ever seen. Presently he appeared on parade, wearing cap and gown, standing in front of the Tin Tab where the School was lined up in forms with their form masters. The School then moved off to the Great Hall for prayers before which Mr Brading came on to the platform to issue the day's instructions in a rich musical voice. He first rang one stroke on the bell and those boys sitting down stood up, he rang two strokes and the Headmaster made his entrance.

The reforms of Henderson were rather too much for Brading. He had been appointed to the staff of the Lower College of God's Gift in 1881 and was the first to hold the post of Second Master of Alleyn's School. His retirement in 1922 was an emotional occasion. An Old Boy who owned the Edison Bell Record Company made a recording of him singing 'Forty Years On' and 'My Friend John' which he had sung at school concerts for years. The boys gave him a suitcase as a retirement present and, in his farewell speech, he said that he could not give all the boys suitcases but would give advice to suit all cases.

1931

1946

1997

E. C. BROWN

E. C. BROWN was the youngest of the six original Housemasters and the only one of them to have seen active service in the Great War. He was a tall, big-boned man whose footsteps used to echo round the School as he strode about, usually carrying under his arm a large mark book bulging with loose papers. He took a leading part in the organisation of games and in the Corps. In the class-room he taught Latin. He had tremendous energy and enthusiasm for athletics but sometimes, in class, he would drop his voice and speak to the boys in confidential tones: "Of course, some people think, but I.....", or "I don't mind personally, but the Head says....." Boys knew he did not see eye to eye with his colleagues, or they with him. The boys returned after the summer holiday in 1925 to find that he had left the School. Rumour was rife and it was supposed he had been in financial difficulties. The boys were sorry he had gone and showed a good deal of loyalty towards him.

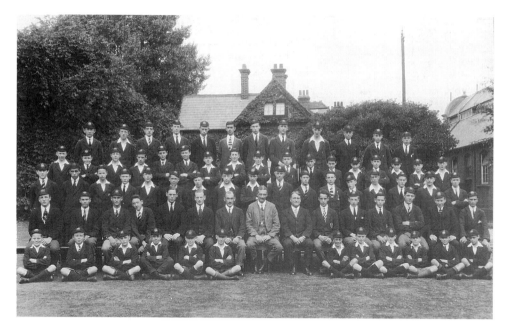

1924

1946

1997

A. E. CRIBB

HE had no nickname, he was called "Mr Cribb" by everyone. He was always immaculately dressed and was quietly spoken. He never hurried and was easily moved to smile behind his round spectacles. He taught English and Mathematics to Middle School boys but seldom called anyone by his actual name. He addressed a class as "Boys", pronounced "Byes" and individuals were called "What's name" which sounded like "Wozneem". He was known to say "Take this book to Mr Woozneem, please Wozneem". He succeeded Brading as Second Master and his quiet tact, perfect manners, humanity and humour must have made him a very important link between Henderson and the staff. Henderson said of Cribb that he was one of the finest men he had ever known. Without him the school could never have expanded and developed as it did.

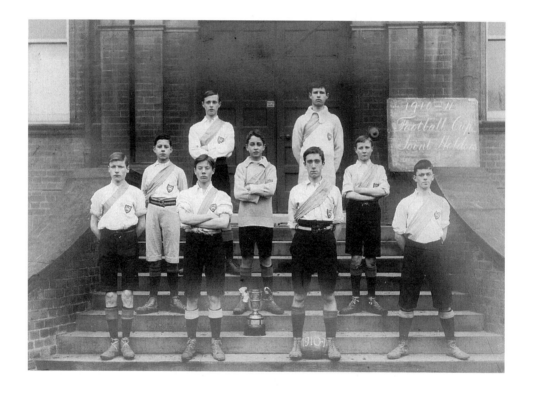

Soccer 1910-1911

c. 1929

1997

F. DUTTON

F. DUTTON was the Senior Chemistry Master. He was seldom seen without a trilby hat which he always wore at a rakish angle even when teaching in the laboratory. He was a first class scientist and teacher. The School's Chemistry Labs were unusually well equipped for those days and year after year Alleyn's boys won awards to Oxford and Cambridge. He knew most boys in the School as he sold dinner tickets before morning school: 9d (green) for cold meat and sweet; 1/- (red) for a hot meal (*note: 1/- =5p*) Nothing could have been a surer sign of his standing in the School than when Henderson asked him to be one of the two Founder Housemasters for the New Houses in 1921, for Henderson never had any preference for Scientists. During the Christmas holidays in 1922 Frank Dutton was suddenly taken ill with pneumonia. He died on 3rd January, 1923.

1929

1948

1998

A. J. ROPER

IN 1873 A. J. Roper became an Assistant Master of the Lower College of God's Gift He moved with Alleyn's to Townley Road in 1887 and continued his work there until he died at the age of 76. He was unfailingly courteous, had an unswerving devotion to duty and possessed skills at all sorts of games. He had a perennial youthfulness which was the envy of his younger colleagues. At an age when others retired, he set about creating and organising Roper's House. He intended to retire at the age of 73 but the Great War deferred this. When too stiff for cricket he took up golf which he was playing in the Summer of 1918 when his health began to fail. He died in February 1919. His funeral service was held in the School Chapel.

1918

c. 1931

1998

51

J. F. SPURGEON

J. F. SPURGEON had been on the staff only three years when he was appointed one of the Founder Housemasters. He held this post for just two years leaving in 1909 to become Headmaster of a Preparatory School in Suffolk. He helped to establish fives as a prominent game at the School and his help with the 1st XI cricket was invaluable. His kindness to those in need and his thoughtful criticism of boys, when he knew it was needed, were his strength. Numerous presentations were made to him at his farewell supper. He was well liked by the boys but his time at the School was insufficient for him to become a 'character'. His name, however, was cemented in House History. At his departure Spurgeon's House presented him with a sports bag and the 1st XI gave him a signed cricket bat.

League Winners 1908

1930

c. 1993

S. J. S. TULLEY

S.J.S. TULLEY was one of the real Old Guard. He stuck to the methods he had always used and boys had to toe the line in every detail. In his earlier years at School he took an active part in cricket and was a dangerous left-hand bowler. Although his interest in the game remained unabated, he was restricted to coaching and umpiring in his later years as he had become decidedly lame. A story went around the School that he had a cork leg. One boy, R. A. Leeming, was determined to test the truth of this story and so stuck the point of a geometrical compass into it. It seems that Leeming had tested the wrong leg!

Tulley used to chew tobacco and he always wore the same type of dark brown tweed suit. He had not been to a university and was one of the few non-graduates to teach at Alleyn's at that time. Boys remembered him for his patient and persistent thoroughness. He never skimped his work, he never hurried his explanations, he never allowed slip-shod work to pass. A 'natural' schoolmaster, he served the School diligently for thirty-one years.

c. 1931

54

1961

1993

C. F. TYSON

CHARLES TYSON was a Lancastrian who combined his north country accent with beautiful diction. This was heard not only in his teaching and announcements but also in his fine baritone voice at many of the pre-war concerts. He came to the School in 1911 and was one of the two Housemasters who served in the 1914-18 War. Whilst on service in France he was awarded the Croix de Guerre and was Mentioned in Dispatches.

'Tyke' had been Centre Half in an English amateur international team and was in charge of School soccer for many years. His subject was French which he taught with great patience and precision. He was a big man but very gentle in his ways. He always had a smile and time to talk, even to the smallest boy in his House. He hardly ever punished anybody. No one thought of taking a liberty with him, he was too much of a gentleman.

By a margin of many years, he was the last surviving Founder-Housemaster. During the Second World War he set up and then organised the South London Emergency Secondary School, which was within Alleyn's buildings, for four and a half years. He was its Second Master when it opened in 1940 and became its Head for the second half of the war. He finally retired in 1947 as Joint Second Master of Alleyn's School.

1929

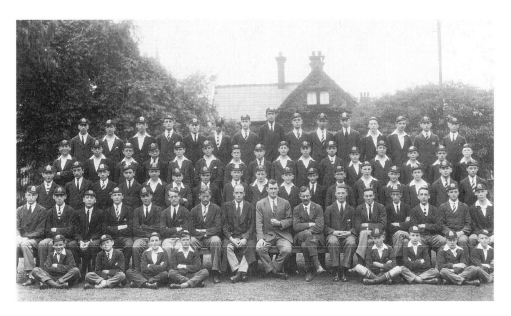

c. 1925

1993

Helm

R.B. Henderson and Staff, c.1934

R.B. HENDERSON, 1920–1940

IN the Summer of 1920 R.B.H. arrived at Alleyn's having previously been Headmaster of Strand School. The Summer holiday was lengthened to equal that of the College and from the start of the Advent Term there was a six day rather than a five day week. Tuesday and Thursday afternoons were allocated to sport and on most Saturdays there were School or House Matches at which attendance was virtually compulsory. Henderson had been a Master at Rugby in his earlier days and was inspired by Thomas Arnold's ideal of educating Christian gentlemen. At one interview he told an applicant for a teaching post "It will be BOYS you will teach here, not Subjects". Parents were told that "the whole waking time of the boy belonged to the School".

In 1921 two further Houses were added to accommodate an increasing number of boys and make inter-House knock-out competitions easier. These Houses were given to F. Dutton , who had been acting Housemaster of Brown's during the 1914-18 War, and to C.F. Tyson. The House Colour of the former was to be dark blue and that of the latter light blue. At the same time Roper's changed from orange to yellow. Mr Dutton died suddenly, as already mentioned, in January 1923.

The Junior School building, constructed in wood, was to take its place at the north east edge of the playing fields. Here Albert Spring, Headmaster of the Lower School, was to mould the young intake for many years to come.

The Organ was installed in 1922 and the War Memorial Panels beneath it were unveiled by Colonel Kirby, VC, AOB. The Organ had to be built in the existing roof space but, as this area proved to be insufficient, an addition had to be made to allow for the installation of pipes.

Henderson thoroughly supported the uniformed Cadet Corps and in 1923 the O.T.C. was duly inaugurated. In 1925, next to the Junior School, an Orderly Room and an Armoury were built. The Rifle Range was added in 1931.

Henderson worked at the academic side emphasising Oxford and Cambridge, often to the annoyance of some of the senior staff who were from London University. No longer did boys leave to complete their education at the College - the Sixth Form was sending its own scholars to the Universities. Matriculation and Higher Schools Certificates were the order of the day. In under ten years Ralph Bushell Henderson had created a "Public School" - in 1929 he was elected to membership of the Headmasters' Conference which distinction has been given to all successive occupants of the Head's Study. His was an unusual study for, in those days, it had a bathroom attached to it!

The House system was encouraged further as the years went by. House colours appeared in most garments of school uniform. Originally the House colour had been shown on the black school cap by a circle of ribbon, now the front and rear sections of each cap were made of coloured cloth, the badge containing a chevron and three cinque foils only.

A School shop was opened upon the arrival of Henderson and it had an 'arrangement' whereby the school had a percentage of the profits. From 1929, the shop became the School's 'very own'. Every item sold in the school shop was

School, c. 1920

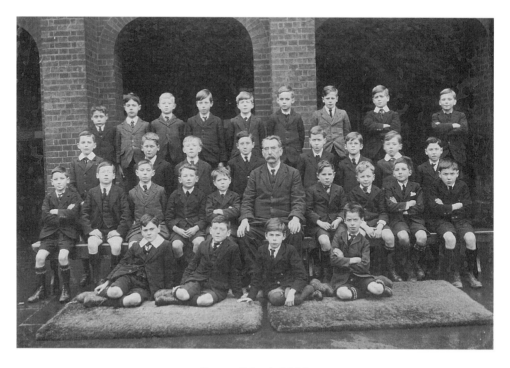

Lower School, 1920

From the Air, c. 1930

stated to be cheaper than elsewhere and all profits were to be returned to the School in one form or another.

Although not designated by colours on the uniform, all members of the Junior School were put into their own Houses. There were four such Junior Houses: Smith's, Baker's, Collins' and Henderson's. The names commemorated the first four Headmasters of the School.

The year 1932 was the fiftieth birthday of Alleyn's. That year saw the consolidation of the Alleyn's School Fund Association which was to "provide amenities which could not be provided by the authorities supplying the money for strictly educational purposes". *The Chestnut Tree* was published for the first time and, although it did not run for many editions, it enabled boys to publish their literary items under a different editorship from the Magazine. It was run by the boys.

J. Laughlin (Tyson's) was School Captain and had the task of re-organising the Prefect System so that there was a real difference between the School Prefects and the House Prefects. It fell to him to exclude the House Prefects from the School Prefects' Room. Laughlin won a Choral Scholarship to Corpus Christi, Cambridge. It is believed that he was the first Old Boy from the School to study Medicine there.

The Edward Alleyn Magazine had a new heading on its contents page that summer, Albert Spring retired as Commanding Officer of the O.T.C., the Masters took a cut in salary because of the country's financial crisis and the new arrivals included a nervous young boy called A.S. Jenkins. J.V.H. Coates, an Old Boy educated in the Village buildings and a Master at the School, was elected President of the Alleyn Old Boys' Club for the Jubilee Year. (See photograph opposite).

Long Jump, 1931

Jubilee Year Dinner (J.V.H. Coates in the Chair)

Henderson, who had had an accident in the Summer holidays of 1931 and had been on sick leave during the Advent Term, returned in January, 1932, full of vigour with further plans for expansion. The wilderness at the junction of Calton Avenue and Townley Road was cleared and levelled. His attention then went to the higher level of Townley Field where it was decided to create a school running track. This was supervised by S.R. Hudson, Master in charge of games, and was constructed by the boys themselves. In the working parties of boys were young Stephen Jenkins and Ken Spring (both to become Masters in later years) under such prefects as Stuart Blanch (to become Archbishop of York). In 1934 new fives courts were erected and in 1935 a new Terrace Pavilion completed the running track area.

In March, 1934, the Headmaster attended a special ceremony at Lambeth Palace where, in the presence of several visitors from the School, the Archbishop of Canterbury conferred upon him the Lambeth Degree of Bachelor of Divinity in recognition of his work as a Biblical scholar in general and of his work *The Four Witnesses* in particular. This was an extremely unusual honour for a layman.

In 1936 a new building, to house the buttery on the ground floor and the library above, was opened. It was placed between the old fives courts and the wooden buildings of the Junior School. One corner of it was overshadowed by the chestnut tree in the corner of the Quad.

Buttery and Library   *Rutherford*

Building the Running Track

Grant of Arms to the Foundation, 1936

Also in 1936 a new Coat of Arms was granted to the whole Foundation of God's Gift. The crest previously used had been that of the family of Edward Alleyn, and the College of Arms decided that, in order to regularise such use, some slight alterations would have to be made. The new description was "Argent a Chevron between three Cinquefoils Gules: a Chief Ermine, thereon a Cinquefoil of the second". Badges on caps, crests on notepaper, and bookplates had to be altered. The new badge was a further sign of progress and independence. However, Henderson decided to use the secondary motto, set above the Coat of Arms on the 1936 Grant of Arms, as the motto of Alleyn's School and he placed it *under* the badge for all reproductions on matters concerning Alleyn's. At the same time he declared that "Townley Road" should never appear on the address of the School "as everybody knows where Alleyn's is".

Badge chosen by Henderson

On 2nd September, 1939, the School left West Dulwich Station for an unknown destination which turned out to be a group of villages around the Maidstone area. Boxley, Detling, Sandling and Weavering were to be the homes of groups of boys for the next sixteen months. The Junior School became known as St Clare when it moved to Walmer and took over a Preparatory School there for a short time.

Henderson had taken the School to the "safety" of mid-Kent, his work in Dulwich was completed and in October, 1940, he became Manchester Reader of Divinity at New College, Oxford. In his final sermon to the School he said ". . . you will not be content with anything short of the highest. You will strive to make this Alleyn's even greater and better, you will never rest content till it is known to you all to be in truth a corner of the Kingdom of God".

School Magazine Cover during the Headships of Henderson, Hudson & Lloyd

OTC Going to Camp

C. R. Allison

C. R. ALLISON, 1940–1945

RALPH ALLISON became Headmaster while the evacuated part of the School was at Maidstone (Seniors) and Rogerstone, Monmouthshire (Juniors). He set about the task of finding a place "somewhere in England" where the whole evacuated School could be together. Rossall School at Fleetwood in Lancashire was willing to share its premises and so on 6th January, 1941, Ralph Allison led his School to the North-West coast.

The Houses were redivided as numbers were smaller than they had been in Dulwich, or even at Maidstone originally. Brading's and Tulley's became Crescent House under Major Hudson, Cribb's and Roper's became Rose House under L.H. Jones, Brown's and Dutton's were The Hall under R.L. Taylor, and Spread Eagle House consisted of Spurgeon's and Tyson's with B.E.G. Davies as the Housemaster. He, however, was soon to leave to join the Forces to which F.A. Meerendonk, E.L. Franklin and S. Incledon had already departed. The new Housemaster was Sir John Maitland who went straight to Rossall from Dulwich where he had been helping C.E. Hack and C.F. Tyson to 'hold the fort' and start the Emergency School for those who had remained behind. James House was the name given to the Junior School which remained under the supervision of Albert Spring.

Rossall School Quad

Allison and School at Rossall

Circumstances had turned part of Alleyn's into a Boarding School. What started as an experiment soon proved its worth. Community spirit and willingness to overcome all sorts of hardships fostered a new way of life for all the boys and many of the staff. Services in the Chapel became a focal point and in addition to formal School worship voluntary services held on Wednesday evenings were well supported and filled a genuine need.

All the sports and clubs previously held in London continued at Rossall. All flourished for now "all the boys waking hours belonged to the School" (what joy for R.B.H.!). There were additional activities such as gardening and "Dig for Victory", ably inspired by V.K. Haslam. Much more drama was organised in which the Headmaster himself often took a leading role. These were peaceful occupations and helped to fill in weekends, holidays and even evenings after prep. The rugged Lancashire coastline with hardly a tree in sight was a far cry from the grounds of the School in leafy Dulwich.

Wartime occupations were essential, reminding the School of the reasons for its exile. A Home Guard Platoon was formed from Masters and Senior Boys under a Sergeant-Major from Rossall. Exercises took place at all hours and normal parades were early in the morning before lessons commenced.

The records of 1942 prove interesting reading concerning the movement of Old Boys. In that year Bertram Simpson became Bishop of Southwark, Harold Bradfield became Archdeacon of Croydon, A.S. Jenkins obtained his degree at Cambridge, J.A.Lanchbery won the Henry Smart Composition Scholarship to the Royal Academy of Music and P.J. Woodfield, who was editor of *The Edward Alleyn Magazine*, left School after obtaining a Special Army Entrance (R.A.). Forty years later Philip Woodfield received the K.C.B. Later still he became Deputy President of the Club but ill health prevented him from undertaking the Presidency.

Exchange visits took place during the Summer. Those at Rossall visited Townley Road for Speech Day and some Old Boys visited Rossall for Founder's Day which was held on a *Friday* in order not to coincide with Rossall's own Speech Day on the Saturday. The Old Boys were led by C.S. Herridge, who had been School Captain two years before the First World War. A general invitation was issued to any Old Boys who could make a visit at any time. Overnight accommodation was made available and many serving in the Forces paid visits while passing through when stationed nearby.

The Alleyn Old Boys' Club began experiencing many difficulties in keeping in contact with its members when two members of school staff came to its rescue. Throughout the days of conflict the Acting Honorary Treasurer was Albert Spring who kept in touch with hundreds of Club Members by adding a personal note whenever he sent a receipt. He encouraged all leavers to become Life Members and, by sending the forms to Charles Tyson, managed to keep track of leavers from the Dulwich contingent. The other record that became a labour of love and honour was that of those serving in His Majesty's Forces and, as must happen in times of war, those who were killed on active service. This was undertaken by Sir John Maitland with meticulous care and to him fell the task of producing the Roll of Honour at the cessation of hostilities.

Cricket Team at Rossall

Rossall School Chapel

Domestic Staff

Rehearsal at Rossall, 1944 (J.A. Smith conducting, W.J. Smith watching)

During the year House Notes for The Hall had listed not a House Captain but 'Secretary to the Committee'. Had the comradeship of war gone too far? The actual Notes were one line: "Happy is the country that has no history". The revolution was not long lived and in October the House returned to the prefectorial system.

The wives of the Masters were very active, helping out in many ways and acting as 'Aunts' to the boys under their husbands' care. Those in the Junior School will ever remember Mrs Spring who took an individual interest in every one of the members of James House and continued to follow their welfare long after they had entered the Senior School.

During the Christmas holidays in 1942 Major Hudson married Miss Barbara Farrow of Sandling near Maidstone. At least some good had come out of the School's evacuation.

By now the School had its own "talkie/movie" projector and fortnightly film shows were a welcome addition. The outside world was not forgotten and in March 1943 an International Forum was held over a full weekend with speakers from seven different countries. This was hosted jointly with Rossall School with whom relations had become not just helpful but very friendly. Alleyn's had not become isolated at Fleetwood, it had become part of the community, associating itself with local events and special war efforts. In Fleetwood's 'Wings for Victory' and 'Salute the Soldier' weeks Alleyn's played its full part. During half terms and some of the holidays, the boys would help on local farms and really proved their worth.

Clothes rationing was hitting hard and, by October 1943, House soccer shirts were in very short supply. An urgent appeal went out to the Old Boys asking them to return any House shirts in their possession to the School for the use of the present generation. Parcels arrived by return. The correct attire was available once more. House Ribbons for straw boaters were becoming unobtainable and were being made of three different coloured ribbons sewn together. Only a few pairs of old stock striped trousers remained in the School Shop.

On 24th March, 1944, the School Orchestra and Choir broadcast on the BBC Home Service. Prepared under the direction of W.J. Smith, some items were conducted by boys. In August the Music Department arranged an impressive Memorial Service for those who had, so far, given their lives in the War.

D-Day meant the end was in sight but the summer was to be unusual. V weapons were falling on London so Speech Day was held in Rossall's Hall. When Trinity Term ended there was a six day break before a new invention, Lammas Term, began. This extra term had a lighter scheme of working hours and a system of directed recreation was introduced to alleviate the burden of the long stay up north.

The lengthy occupation of the Rossall Houses was causing difficulties for the host School and therefore new accommodation had to be found. Throughout the war there had been a slow but continuous two-way traffic of boys - some wanted to 'go home' and therefore returned to Dulwich with education at Townley Road, a few 'did not like the bombs' and left London for Rossall. By 1944 Alleyn's numbers in Lancashire had declined considerably.

With the increase in the numbers of Rossall School itself, the Alleyn's Houses moved out to residences in Fleetwood. Rose House took over Watson's Hotel while Spread Eagle and The Hall shared the Cumberland Hotel. The disadvantage of early morning rising to catch the bus was easily compensated for by the luxury of hotel bedrooms with hot and cold water!

The Home Guard stood down on 2nd December and all realised, some with mixed feelings, that the days at Rossall were numbered. The Lent Term of 1945 went very quickly. On 26th March the sun shone, "Alleyn's weather" as the natives of those parts had learned to call it over the past four years, and the boys entered Big School for a combined final assembly. The two School Captains, Cranfield of Alleyn's and Peters of Rossall, expressed genuine feelings of mutual respect and goodwill in farewell speeches. The two Headmasters echoed the same sentiments which the two Schools endorsed with cheers for each other. Parting gifts were announced - Rossall was to present Alleyn's with an inter-House Cricket Trophy to be known as the "Rossall Shield" and Alleyn's would send to Rossall (when they could be bought) wooden seats for "The Square" such as the Rossallians had often envied the Alleyn's boys using during their stay. Approximately two hundred boys and staff left Rossall and came, led by Mr Allison, to the "Promised Land".

Cross Country Running at Rossall

C.F. Tyson, Headmaster of SLESS

THE WAR YEARS IN DULWICH

MEANWHILE, in Dulwich, The South London Emergency Secondary School quickly to be known as SLESS, was housed in Alleyn's buildings from March 1940 to March 1945. For six months retired Alleyn's Masters and others had educated those not evacuated in private houses and local halls. Henderson felt that the boys in London should have a proper education and sent Hack and Tyson to re-open the Alleyn's building. This was undertaken not only to educate Alleyn's boys who wished to remain in London but also, in conjunction with the London County Council Education Department, to offer a Grammar School education to others whose schools were evacuated but did not themselves wish to leave London. SLESS kept Alleyn's buildings alive.

On the Roll were boys from seventeen schools and eleven masters from six schools. The Acting Headmaster was C.E. Hack and the Second Master C.F. Tyson. From Alleyn's staff came Evans, McClymont, Crewe and Rudd - the old names were there to show the way. The Alleyn's House System was started immediately and the new School was divided into eight Houses:

Evan's House was brown	Crewe's House was green
Allison's House was mauve	Fowler's House was dark blue
Rudd's House was yellow	Wright's House was pink
Bryant's House was red	McClymont's House was light blue

Games were played, fives was taught to newcomers and holidays were filled in with "Holiday Clubs".

Mr Hack was soon confirmed as Headmaster and the first SLESS School Captain, A.K. Cooper (McClymont's & Tyson's) was appointed in 1941 when, of the 240 boys attending, 114 belonged to Alleyn's. Sports were soon well under way on the fields that could be used. Some became unusable as the old elm trees were felled by blast. Out of commission for the whole of the war was the Townley Field as new brick and concrete buildings appeared to house the R.A.F. barrage balloon crews. Underground shelters were dug between the running track and the houses in Woodwarde Road for use by local residents. The huge balloon overshadowed the main building at times and, more than once, nearly settled on the School's roof. Huge National Savings Campaigns were organised and the Junior Training Corps, under Captain M.Crewe, had enthusiastic enrolment.

Academic work was, however, the main reason for attendance and this was not forgotten. On some days more lessons would be taken in the basement (the air raid shelter) than in the classroom, owing to enemy air activity. All staff had to undertake fire watching at nights and at the weekends.

In 1942 C.L. Spittle (Fowler's & Dutton's) became School Captain. The General Schools Certificate was undertaken in the most unusual conditions, bombs dropping and lights failing. Twenty-four took the exam, fourteen obtained Matriculation exemption and five the Certificate. By now there were 400 boys and 14 forms. In the summer some 'visitors' appeared in order to hold their Speech Day. It seemed they had come from a place called "Rossall".

Bomb damage -
The Chapel Tower

Bomb damage -
Dulwich Picture
Gallery

*Bomb damage -
Chapel Gallery*

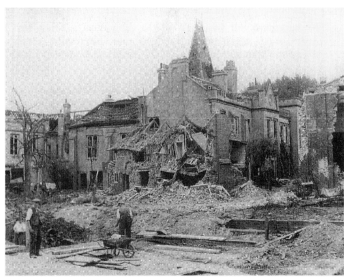

*Bomb damage -
Foundation buildings
from Gallery Road*

In January 1943 M. Miller (Highbury Grammar School) became School Captain. At the same time the younger boys belonging to The Strand School returned to their own building, now re-opened for full time education, but others came to take their place. As the War continued boys drifted back to London all the time. Messrs Hutt, Wright and Eayrs of Alleyn's had joined SLESS from Rossall or the Forces.

In the Summer of 1943 Mr W. Anderson (St Dunstan's College) died suddenly in the Common Room. This, even in war, sent sadness through the School. It was his School that provided the next School Captain, J.H.M Ellis. For ten weeks from mid-July to mid-September, SLESS ran its own harvest camp at Hartfield in Sussex under the direction of Mr J. Logan. There were now five mistresses on the staff and they were given their own Common Room situated immediately to the right of the main entrance.

A mid-term Service was held at the Chapel in the Summer and School Services were held there at least once a term thereafter. Once more the visitors came from Rossall to hold their Speech Day and Alleyn's Staff at Dulwich joined those from Rossall on the platform for this occasion - a recognition that the two were really one.

In October, Mr Allison spent a week at the School in Townley Road. He was able to see the building to which his School belonged and also speak to the Alleyn's boys who had chosen not to leave London. At Christmas the School said goodbye to Mr Hack upon his retirement and to Miss M.C. Gaukrodger who was to be married. She had been the first woman ever to teach in the building.

In January 1944 C.F. Tyson became Headmaster and the Roll was 460 strong. The Preacher at the term's Chapel Service was the Bishop of Southwark, The Rt Revd Bertram Simpson, AOB, who expressed his pleasure at the sincerity of the boys. Although the School was living in the midst of War, and every week news was given at Morning Assembly of Alleyn Old Boys being killed, the tragedy was really brought home when it was announced that W.R. Wood of Bec School, a SLESS Prefect who left in 1941, had been killed with the Royal Air Force. The war had come back to London; the Blitz may have been over but now the V weapons had arrived and lessons were again interrupted by air raids. Once more lessons were in the basement rather than above in the form rooms. Many homes of staff and boys were bombed or badly damaged. P.H. Jenkyn (Rudd's & Roper's) of 5A was killed by enemy bombing on 31st July. Fellow pupils were saddened when they were told after the war that Jenkyn's name could not be included on the War Memorial as he had not been killed 'on active service'. Mr Hutt and Mr Rudd, bastions of strength in the consolidation of SLESS, retired at the end of the Summer Term. Mr C.H. Williams, a temporary Master, went to Rossall during the Summer holidays to teach P.E. until a replacement for Mr Heal, who had just retired, could be found. He was then appointed to Alleyn's Staff but returned to teach in the 'Dulwich Division'.

The School learnt to live with doodlebugs and rockets. Through the war years sport had become very strong. The state of the ground that had been so important during 1939-1940 seemed to be of little importance now, it was the game, the exercise, a few visits and the camaraderie that counted. There were

SLESS Staff, 1945

matches every Saturday with Mr Rees in charge of the Seniors and Mr Pritchard taking special care of the Juniors.

Clubs within the School also flourished. The Forum Club organised a public debate at the end of the Autumn Term on the motion "That co-education would benefit Alleyn's School". Dr E L Giles was in the Chair for this historic debate (believed to be the first time that 'co-education' and 'Alleyn's' were mentioned at the same time). The motion, however, was defeated. Extracts from *Macbeth* and a one act play *The Dear Departed* were presented. Before the performance the audience was told that if an air raid warning sounded the performance would continue unless the look-outs on the roof sounded their whistles when all would evacuate to the basement as quickly as possible. The Stage Manager for the production was A.C. Bate (Bryant's & Tulley's), the School Captain, who later became School Captain of Alleyn's and later still a Major-General.

George Swift, AOB, already mentioned in this history, paid daily visits to the School. He watched all the games and from time to time would tell the boys of his own schooldays in the Village, of how and when the School buildings were erected, of the Army and above all of the heritage that belonged to the School. He was part of SLESS but, more importantly, he was the living history of the Alleyn Foundation and was looked upon by staff and pupils alike as the authority in all things concerning the School's history and traditions. It was from 1944 until 1948 that the current author, as a pupil, listened intently to George Swift. Later, as two AOBs, they would meet in order that the history and traditions were passed on.

In the 1950s George Swift's blazer badge, in a polished oak frame, was used as a prize for Inter-House Sport in Alleyn's Junior School.

As the Allied Armies advanced across Europe, air attacks on London ceased and the time had come for the two parts of Alleyn's to be re-united. Five years and ten days after the first pupils had enrolled for SLESS, this Emergency School completed its task. It was born of War which could have been its weakness. The comradeship of War was its strength and success. Thirty-six masters and mistresses had been on the staff roll, over 1,200 boys coming from twenty-four schools had benefitted from its instruction. In 1945 the majority of boys at the School were members of Alleyn's and, by this time, the majority of the members of Alleyn's were at SLESS as fewer Alleyn's boys returned from Rossall as were already in Dulwich to receive them. Some scholarship holders who were members of other schools applied for transfers to Alleyn's and some returned to their own schools either at Easter or in the September. In March, 1945, SLESS ended and after the Easter holiday a combined roll of those from Rossall and those from London assembled at Alleyn's School for the last term of Mr Allison's Headship. It was not an easy merger. Those from Rossall talked about those from SLESS as "joining Alleyn's School". This struck hard when those from SLESS had to give their returned brethren geographical directions around the Townley Road Building. Alleyn's boys who had been in London throughout the war did not take kindly to the 'intruders'.

A.C.Bate was allowed to remain a Prefect (House only), all other SLESS Prefects were 'reduced to the ranks'. It is interesting to note that four consecutive Alleyn's School Captains from January 1947 had all been 'Alleyn's at SLESS'.

Mr Tyson was made joint Second Master with Major Hudson which was understandable; what could not be understood was why he was only 'joint' Second Master after Hudson became the acting Head.

Some staff who had temporary appointments at SLESS were appointed to Alleyn's where in future years they were to have great influence. They were Dr E.L. Giles who taught English and was Library Master, J. Logan who became Housemaster of Tyson's and Commanding Officer of the CCF, P.C.Phillips who taught Geography, D.H.B. Pritchard who succeeded A. Spring as Headmaster of the Lower School, Miss T. Ratzer who taught Art, H.I.T. Rees who taught Mathematics, Miss D. Wiggs who was the first woman to be 'permanently' appointed to Alleyn's Staff, and C.H. Williams who became Head of Physical Education.

Mr Tyson wrote of SLESS: "Our last service of dismissal in the School Hall was a solemn and sincere business for all. Cheers and rejoicing were naturally out of place, but, mixed with regret, there was a note of satisfaction both in the knowledge of a job well done and in the resolve to put forth every effort to help in the days of reconstruction which lie ahead."

Crest of the London County Council

Allison and Staff amalgamated in Dulwich, Summer Term 1945

S.R. HUDSON, 1945–1963

THE AFTERMATH OF WAR - two schools, trained in different environments, now joined but not yet one. Ralph Allison was headmaster in Dulwich for only one term as, while at Rossall, he had already accepted the headship of Brentwood School as from Advent Term 1945. The School which he left was put under the control of S.R. Hudson (otherwise known as "George" or "Soapy") who became Acting Headmaster in September 1945, the position being confirmed in 1947. Three questions faced the new Head - Could there be a real amalgamation of the Rossall and Dulwich sections of the School? How could we remember those who had been killed in the War and repay our debt to them? and What was going to happen to the School, would it become an L.C.C. Grammar School, would it disappear or would it remain independent?

Immediately he set about tackling the first question. From serving in the Forces, came Masters unknown to both sets of boys. In turn, these Masters did not know where the boys had spent the war years. Sports, School Clubs, dining by Houses, the Sixth Form being divided by subjects - all these helped to make one school although some unfortunate barriers were to remain, obviously due to valid educational reasons, for instance Remove A (Rossall) became VA at Alleyn's, Remove A (SLESS) became VC at Alleyn's. By September 1946 the name changes meant nothing - the Schools were united. As already stated the four School Captains appointed from January 1947 onwards had never seen Rossall - A.C. Bate (Tulley's), L.F. Walker (Brown's) and J.F. Maple (Brown's) were from SLESS whilst R. Birmingham (Spurgeon's) joined the School after the return.

Hudson answered the second question at Speech Day, 1946, when he said that the debt to those who had been killed could be repaid "by making certain that the ideals for which they died are achieved." A War Memorial Fund was set up, the result of which was twofold. Firstly, four further panels were added to the existing memorial under the organ loft in the Great Hall and, secondly, a War Memorial Garden was created on the triangle of ground at the junction of Townley Road and Calton Avenue where the R.A.F. Barrage Balloon Site had been during the War. The field side of this triangle was roughly to follow "Smith's Walk" first trodden in 1887. The Garden was designed and created by Mr V.K. Haslam, a master from 1927 until 1955. Gardening and weeding had been Mr Haslam's holiday and spare time occupation for himself and boys while at Rossall but now he was able to devote a life's experience into turning a rough, useless corner of the Townley Field into a beautiful and inspiring Memorial to the Old Boys as well as a pleasant sight to all who pass by.

A Memorial Service for those who had died was held in the Chapel on 29th March 1947. The Roll of Honour consisting of one hundred and thirteen names was read by Mr A. Spring (Headmaster of the Junior School), Mr A.F. Day (President of the Old Boys' Club) and Mr C.R. Allison (Wartime Headmaster of the School).

The Anthem "Requiem Aeternam" was specially composed for the occasion by John Lanchbery, AOB (now a world famous conductor) and the bass soloist

S.R. Hudson

was David Franklin, AOB (later to become a principal at Covent Garden Opera House) Another Old Boy, the Rt Revd Harold Bradfield, Bishop of Bath and Wells, gave the address.

The War Memorial Panels in the Great Hall were not unveiled until Founder's Day, 1949, by which time 124 names had been inscribed thereon. The ceremony was performed by Major-General Sir Leslie Williams, KBE, CB, MC, AOB, after which the additional oak panels were dedicated and blessed by The Bishop of Southwark, the Rt Revd B.F. Simpson, MC, AOB.

In 1949, for the first time, Alleyn's was represented in the Public Schools Cricket at Lords when M.J. Stewart (Tulley's) played for Southern Schools v the Rest. He was awarded the Public Schools Cap for playing for them against the Combined Services team.

In July, after twenty-nine years on the staff, Sir John Maitland retired. He taught Classics and had been Housemaster of Spurgeon's since 1928. He had been an inspiration to many and a mine of accurate information and scholarly knowledge on such subjects as Scottish Jurisprudence, Roman and Restoration Drama or the "doings" of the Army of Salonika. He was not to have a long retirement, for he died in November, aged seventy years.

Cricket on the Pavilion Pitch
Picture shoes 'Tin Tab' in the centre and Wooden Junior School to the right

Hudson and Prefects, Trinity Term 1946

For forty years Albert Spring had been an influential force in the School. he was appointed in 1909 and, except for four years' service in the R.F.C. (later the R.A.F.) had taught in the Junior School. Under Henderson he became the Headmaster of the Junior School though this did not stop him taking part in Senior School activities. He was an active Officer and former C.O. of the Corps, a post that his son, Ken, was to hold some years later. He was acting treasurer of the Old Boys' Club during the war years and always encouraged boys to join the Club while still at school. It was he who collected Life Subscriptions by instalments. His wife was a professional musician and always put her talents at the service of the School. Mr Spring retired from Alleyn's at the end of the Trinity Term, 1949. The Alleyn Old Boys' Club elected him President and at the 1950 Dinner, at which he presided, he was pleased to instal one of "his boys" ('Young' Bradfield, the Bishop of Bath and Wells) as his successor. He was succeeded as Headmaster of the Junior School by D.H.B. Pritchard.

At about this time the School's CCF Band was formed as a full sized Military Band and it was decided that a competition should be held in order to find a suitable School March. The first section in E(b) was the winning entry which was submitted by C.H. Jaeger, later to become Lieut.-Colonel Jaeger, Director of Music at Kneller Hall. Subsequently, Alleyn's School Bandmaster, A.E. Cave, AOB, decided that the march was too short and added the trio section in A(b). The name of the composer was never shown on the instrument parts for the School March.

Cricket Team, 1947

Music Performance under Frank Kennard

The Corps on a Route March
Captain Taylor, R.S.M. Bate, Lieutenant Jenkins

War Memorial Garden - Crest over Entrance Gates

War Memorial Rose Garden

Before the Second World War the Corps had a very active drum and trumpet band and therefore it is possible that the drum link is older than the March itself and dates from that earlier period. Alan Cave had, as a boy, played in the drum and trumpet band, which possessed a complete set of drums including two marching bass drums with the School Badge on them, a mace and bugles. After the War, so rumour has it, the School came by a complete set of military band instruments which had previously belonged to the Free Polish Army and were "recovered" from a store near Hammersmith Bridge. When the First Surrey Rifles were disbanded, their silver mace and bugles were presented to the School Corps. These instruments were used regularly throughout the fifties and sixties. A regular engagement was on Remembrance Sunday when the Band played for Q Battery RA (TA) and headed their March Past. Nearly twenty years after its formation the full Military Band headed the Procession for the Dulwich Millennium Procession in 1967, playing the School March, and afterwards played all the music required for the three hour Pageant.

Trio

Trumpets   Trumpets

Drum link

Side drum
Bass drum

95

The Summer of 1951 included two fascinating events, one looking backwards and the other, however unwittingly, looking forward. On Speech Day, Mr Henderson, a former Headmaster, was the Guest of Honour and he spoke on the educational system coming from the inspiration of Arnold of Rugby as he had spoken in the same hall thirty years before. A week later there was a never-to-be-forgotten open air performance of *Julius Caesar*. Taking place in Mussolini's Rome, with air and army contingents of the CCF being the Roman Soldiers, this massive presentation was produced by a Master who had joined the staff two years earlier. His name was Michael Croft. Anthony was played by Julian Glover and Artemidorus was John Stride. Here on the playing field between the Pavilion and Townley Road seeds were sown and acting partnerships started that were to blossom in future years into the National Youth Theatre.

The third question that had faced Hudson when he became Head was still unanswered. Plans were afoot to take the Townley and Terrace Fields and build a state school on them. The wits of the day had already named it "Townley Road Secondary". Hudson fought for the continuation of Alleyn's, and the preservation of its traditions and eventually won

In July 1951 Mr L.H. ("Bub") Jones retired as Second Master. He had been a boy at the School and joined the staff in 1913. He became Housemaster of Cribb's in 1934 and was made Joint Second Master by Mr Hudson in 1945.

Athletics: School versus AOBs, 1958
AOB Team: J. Maple, T. Higgins and B. Higgins
School Team: Kingdom, Harding and Chaplin

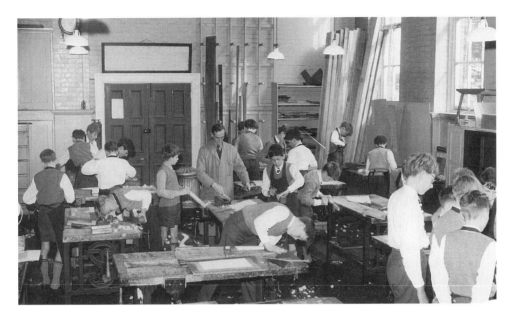

Woodwork Shop with Emrys Evans Teaching

Sidney Incledon was appointed by the Governors to be the next Second Master. This was an excellent choice, for fate decreed that he should be the second-in-command to three headmasters, two of whom were sick men. During illnesses or inter-regnums he acted in their stead.

It was not until 21st June, 1957, that Mr Hudson's fighting spirit was rewarded, for on that day the Secretary of State for Education had agreed that Alleyn's should be added to the list of Direct Grant Schools. His efforts had made the School strong but his own health weak.

He could not plan for the School's future as there were no funds and therefore a massive Appeal Programme was worked out. New buildings were required. Science had outgrown the old labs and the Junior School wooden building with the Tin Tab were showing definite signs of wear. Hudson's appeal produced a 'Plan for the Future'. A new Science Block was in use before he retired. Plans for an additional wing to the main school and a complete new Lower School Building were well in hand.

During Mr Hudson's Headship, the Hough family who for many years had been connected with the School and the Old Boys' Club, sold 8 Dulwich Village to the Estates Governors (they thought they were selling it to the School), so that, for the first time, there was to be an official residence for the Headmaster of Alleyn's.

Major Hudson retired in July, 1963, having served the School since 1926. He had been Head of Geography, Housemaster of Tulley's and Commanding Officer of the OTC under Henderson. He had been appointed Second Master by Allison whilst at Rossall in 1944 and eventually succeeded him four terms later.

Main building, New wing

Spring Building (Lower School)

Rutherford

C.W. LLOYD, 1963–1966

CHARLES LLOYD became Head in September, 1963. The Building Appeal needed more funds in order to bring Hudson's plans to fruition and Mr Lloyd spoke at many meetings and travelled many miles in order to help raise the money for this vital development of the School.

Soon after his arrival heating was centrally provided and the extension block, including the new Common Room, was connected to the main building. In 1964 Stevens, the School Porter, retired after 29 years of service. In March 1965 Lower School pupils quickly settled into the new "Spring" building built between Townley and Hillsboro Roads. The new name commemorated a great Head of what used to be called the Junior School.

On Speech Day that year two Old Boys played prominent parts. Leslie Farrow was the Chairman and Professor R.V. Jones was the Guest of Honour. Mr Lloyd outlined some of the Nuffield Projects in teaching methods which would result in the boys being less spoon-fed in future. He also stressed the need for oral work in the early stages of language learning which would be helped by a new Language Laboratory.

New dining rooms and kitchens had just been completed and were now in use. The first phase of the rebuilding programme which also included the science building was now complete. Work on a new Gymnasium and a Swimming Pool was beginning on the site of the old wooden Lower School and CCF Armoury. The latter had just been rehoused in the basement of the main building with a special grant from the War Office.

More space was needed and, inevitably, another Appeal was launched. More meetings and more travel for Mr Lloyd. He had identified himself with the School, its principles, policies, aims and activities. He was liked by Old Boys, pupils and staff. He was a remarkable Headmaster and was leading Alleyn's to a great future.

It was with astonishment and regret that early in the summer holidays of 1966 the news was heard that Charles Lloyd had accepted from Lord Shawcross, Chairman of the Governors, the unsolicited offer of the Mastership of the other place . . .

The Governors had not been satisfied with the candidates for the vacancy at Dulwich College and decided to offer it to Charles Lloyd. Lord Shawcross telephoned him and gave him twenty-hours to decide, adding the rider "if you decline our offer, this conversation has never taken place". He returns regularly to Alleyn's for Founder's Days and reunions.

Charles Lloyd, Ken Spring (C.O.) and Sydney Incledon with CCF Officers

The Start of the Swimming Pool

The Completed Swimming Pool

Christ's Chapel Entrance

J.L. FANNER, 1967–1975

OWING to the rather sudden departure of Charles Lloyd, the School started the Lent Term in 1967 with Sidney Incledon as Acting Headmaster. It was during this period that preparations were taking place for the Dulwich Millennium Celebrations on 17th June. William Darby, a Master at the College, was Chairman of the Celebrations Committee, but Alleyn Old Boys were responsible for the main event. This was a Pageant depicting various events in the history of Dulwich from the year 967 AD. The Secretary to the Committee and Pageant Producer was Brian Green, AOB. Alleyn's Cadet Force Band with its Bandmaster, Alan Cave, AOB, led the Pageant Procession through the Village. This part of the day was master-minded and marshalled by Eric Randall, Alleyn's School Serjeant. The three hour Pageant was directed and narrated by Arthur R. Chandler, AOB, who also wrote the majority of the script. Over four thousand people watched the performance in the grounds of Belair Mansion.

It was, therefore, to a joyous Dulwich that John Fanner came in September 1967 to become the eighth Headmaster of Alleyn's School. No sooner had he arrived than plans for another celebration were under way. Two years of careful planning preceded the 350th Anniversary of the granting of the Foundation Charter by James I & VI to Edward Alleyn in 1619. This was to be a grand celebration - the 300th had been remembered in the aftermath of The Great War, the 325th had been lost in the turmoil of the last conflict.

In March, 1969, "Faustus" was performed in the Great Hall. This was very appropriate as the play had been written by Christopher Marlowe for Edward Alleyn, and tradition states that it was while acting in this play that Alleyn was confronted by the real Devil and thereupon vowed to found a charitable College.

In the Summer term there were three Royal Visitors to the Foundation. On 12th June H.R.H. The Duke of Edinburgh visited the buildings and planted a commemorative tree and on the following day, H.R.H. Prince George of Denmark carried out the Annual Inspection of the CCF The Archbishop of Canterbury, as Visitor, preached the sermon at the Commemorative Service in the Chapel on 22nd June. There was a Garden Party at the Picture Gallery attended by H.M. Queen Elizabeth the Queen Mother on 9th July, and two days later The Edward Alleyn Ball was held at the Royal Festival Hall.

Visit of H.R.H. The Duke of Edinburgh, 12th June 1969

"A school magazine should reflect the life of the school in all its aspects: work, games, other school activities and (most important of all) the reactions of individual people, both to the school and to other facets of life in general. For various reasons *The Edward Alleyn Magazine* is not entirely suitable for this purpose ..." Thus wrote the new Headmaster in his introduction to *Scriblerus* the new 'School' Magazine first published in 1969. The editors of *The Chestnut Tree* would have been delighted. All aspects of School life were reported and amply illustrated. *The Edward Alleyn Magazine* became the responsibility of the Old Boys and, for the second time in the School's history, there were two different publications, one for the School and one for the Old Boys Club. This time, however, without any animosity between them.

The New Dining Room

1970 was to herald a period of great change for Alleyn's School. In that year a very important benefactor came to the School's assistance and was to become an honoured friend. During the previous year the Government had announced the withdrawal of state support for grant-aided schools and the Clerk to the Worshipful Company of Saddlers drew the Court's attention to the problem that this would cause to Alleyn's School. The Clerk had been made aware of the situation when sitting next to a former headmaster of Alleyn's at a City function. The Saddlers' Company responded at a special Court Meeting held on 1st October when it was agreed "to sponsor Alleyn's School, and to provide funds, not exceeding £25,000 per annum, to fill the gap caused by the withdrawal of the Inner London Education Authority's annual grant to this School". Three weeks later the Master and Clerk of the Saddlers' Company had a meeting with Lord Shawcross, Chairman of the Governors, and the Bursar to the Foundation, at Saddlers' Hall. The connection between the Company and the School was enthusiastically received. The Governors agreed that an existing vacancy on their Board should be offered to the Saddlers' Company who nominated Past Master P.S. McDougall for that honour. Steps were then taken to create another seat on the Board to be held ex-officio by the Master in Office. The Master and the Clerk of the Company attended the Old Boys' Dinner that month in order to cement the link still further.

As the Company's scholarships have been, from the outset, awarded solely on academic merit, Saddlers' Scholars at Alleyn's have made a major contribution in raising the level of the School's academic attainment. The subsequent record of successes in entering higher education reflects credit on the School and the Company whose financial support for scholarships has increased steadily over the years.

Saddlers' Hall

The London Gazette dated Tuesday 23rd May, 1972, announced the award of Membership of the Most Excellent Order of the British Empire to Major Eric Randall for his services to the CCF. He came to the School in January 1948 from the Grenadier Guards to be the Sergeant-Major with the JTC but he soon became involved with many School activities that had nothing to do with the Corps.

He would set up all examination rooms twice a year and his office became the first aid centre of the School. He dealt with dinner tickets, he dealt with lost property, he became involved with many of the extras outside class and House activities from the annual jumble sale to the minute detail required for the Founder's Day programme. His organisational genius had been put at the disposal of Alleyn's and the result was constantly seen in many School and Old Pupils' functions.

At Speech Day in 1972 the Headmaster announced that some candidates would in future be entered for the CSE, as the School clearly had a duty to enter for other public examinations those who had little prospect of success in GCE. He explained that this system had the virtue of easing the academic demands made on the least able boys, at the same time enabling them to acquire qualifications. During the year the Library had been divided so as to provide a separate and specially furnished study centre for the Sixth Form. The new Gymnasium and Swimming Pool were in use and, with the exception of a new Pavilion, the buildings for which the appeal had been launched were now at the service of the boys.

In 1973 Sir John (later Lord) Wolfenden became Chairman of the Board of Governors. At the same time Sir Leonard Hooper, AOB (Roper's), was elected the Alleyn's Common Room Representative on the Board. The Governors had to face inevitable changes in the School's financial position arising from the abolition of Direct Grant Status.

The following year the decision was taken that Alleyn's should become independent and also coeducational thereby giving parents the choice, within the Foundation, of either a single sex or a coeducational school. On the academic side, by doubling the number of potential candidates for entrance to Alleyn's, a higher standard would automatically prevail.

Denise Barber, Veronique Mott, Sarah Utting, Kate Hollingshead and Sarah Hewitt. The First Girls to be Pupils at the School.

In 1974 the new Commanding Officer of the CCF was Lieut.-Colonel A.S. Jenkins, AOB (Roper's), and the Annual Inspection was carried out by Brigadier A.C. Bate, AOB (Tulley's). At the Annual Inspection in 1947 these two Officers were Subaltern and C.S.M. respectively.

During the quarter century that had separated these two Inspections the Music of the School had been under the direction of Frank Kennard, AOB, who retired at the end of the Summer Term. He had guided the School's music through the post-war period and had jealously guarded and upkept the orchestral and Gilbert and Sullivan traditions of the School instilled in it by W. J. Smith.

Other Old Boys were in the news at this time. The death was announced of Air Marshal Sir Walter Pretty, KBE, CB, who had been prominent in the development of Radar during his wartime career. The Birthday Honours List included a Knighthood for Victor Pritchett (V.S. Pritchett), the well-known writer. In May, 1975, the Most Revd and Rt Hon Stuart Blanch, who had been Bishop of Liverpool, was enthroned as Lord Archbishop of York.

A computer laboratory, which had recently been established, took a step forward when a land-line link was introduced. This meant that computers could communicate with other computers on the same land line. This 'wonderful' new method of research could be carried out with ease and economy to any other computer similarly equipped anywhere in London. With demands for a more varied choice in manual subjects, plans were put forward to reorganise the Craft Department. Metal and plastics would need to be catered for but, with the advent of girls in the School, Domestic Science was then the obvious priority.

Denise Barber, Veronique Mott, Sarah Utting, Kate Hollingshead and Sarah Hewitt were the first girls to be pupils at the School. Four came in September, 1975, Veronique followed in January, 1976.

John Fanner died on 15th December, 1975, unexpectedly after a minor operation. He had not lived to see the young girls arriving early in the Lent Term to take the examination for first year entrants. He had appointed four women to the staff and had welcomed the first four of the original girls' Sixth Form.

In spite of failing health, which nobody realised at the time of his appointment, he transformed the School during his eight years as Headmaster. During his stewardship there were many changes in order to allow the pupils to be better prepared for the modern world. The most significant change in the curriculum was the introduction of the Middle School 'block' system in place of the rigid streaming that had existed for seventy years. The new system stated that all pupils must take the basic subjects but then they would be allowed to choose the remainder from an extensive list of options. He had moved the School forward from the post-Victorian era to the latter part of the twentieth century.

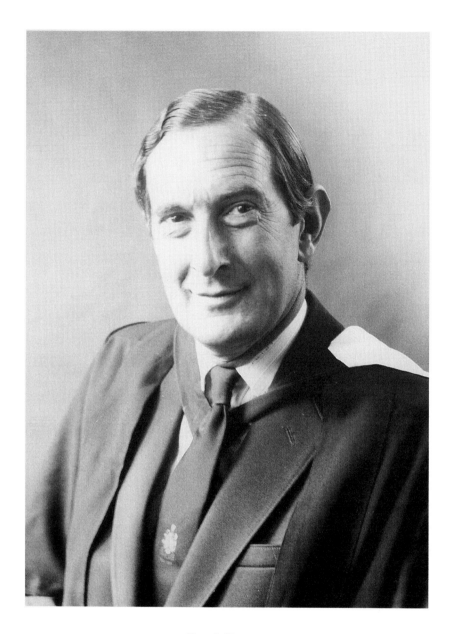

Derek Fenner

D. A. FENNER 1976–1992

ANOTHER interregnum was inevitable and John Newton, who came to the School as Second Master upon the retirement of Sidney Incledon, held the fort for two terms keeping the School in admirable order before the massive changes to come.

At the start of the Advent Term 1976 the School took on fully independent status, it became coeducational with a first year intake that included thirty girls and it had a five day rather than a six day week. The last Headmaster of Alleyn's who had run a five day week was Mr Collins who was educated at Epsom College and Caius College, Cambridge. It so happens that the new Headmaster, Derek Fenner, was also educated at these two seats of learning. Mr Fenner's arrival, so dictated by fate, allowed him to be in at the very start of the new and adventurous schemes for Alleyn's.

Changes were quickly to take place. The Great Hall had new curtains, the oak benches, that had served generations of boys, were sold as souvenirs and replaced by chairs. The War Memorials to both World Wars and the Boer War were resited in the corridor behind the Great Hall while beneath it alterations were made to the arches so that a new Prefects' Room and a Sixth Form Common Room could be created.

Money for school amenities had, for years, been raised by the Social Committee ably led by Reg Hill, AOB with the annual jumble sales organised by Rae Sheppard. These events raised thousands of pounds. In keeping with modern educational thought concerning parental involvement, it was decided to start the 'Alleyn's Association' for parents and friends of the School. Roger Kendrick was the first Chairman and Alistair Hanton the first Secretary. The Social Committee amalgamated with the Association and all fund raising and social activities were then organised under one banner. Dances, book sales, music and theatre groups for parents and some Founder's Day activities came under the Association's wing.

To encourage application for places from a wider area the Headmaster wanted to start coach services to the school. After two false starts an honorary organiser was appointed in late 1978 and three services started in spring 1979. They were from Orpington, Putney and Carshalton. These developed and other routes were added until, after a few years, Alleyn's set up a committee to coordinate the various coach routes run by the Dulwich Schools. This meant that coaches organised by one school would carry pupils from others thus avoiding duplication of routes. Today there are over fifteen coaches controlled by the schools providing a specialised transport service from outlying areas to Dulwich.

In the early years of Mr Fenner's Headship Mr Barker, Housemaster of Cribb's, and Mr McCloy retired. Both had given many years of dedicated service to the School.News of the deaths of Mr Rees and Mr Incledon was received with regret by staff and Old Boys. The Executors of Ivor Rees instituted a Memorial Prize and The Sidney Incledon Bursary Fund was set up by the Edward Alleyn Club. This enables a child to stay on for sixth form education who, for financial reasons, would be unable so to do.

Stuart Blanch, Lord Archbishop of York, 1982

Each year another group of girls entered the school. New toilets, needle-work rooms, changing rooms all appeared at the right times. More ladies joined the staff and Mrs Tessa Cox became the first Senior Mistress. The Combined Cadet Force had girl cadets with their first lady officer, Mrs Pat Barden.

In common with two neighbouring schools, Alleyn's was attacked by an arsonist in March 1980 when one classroom was destroyed in the old Science Block and major computer equipment was damaged beyond repair because of smoke. Temporary classrooms appeared at the end of the Quad (shades of the Tin Tab!) but they lasted only one term while the damage was repaired. Thanks to a group of Old Boy actors led by the former master, Michael Croft, money was raised by a special performance in the Great Hall in aid of the computer replacement fund.

In 1980 two Housemasters retired from their post as Housemaster but not from the School. No longer would a Housemastership be for life - a precedent had been established. Mr J.S. Clarke gave up Brading's after twenty-one years and was followed by Mr I.P. Davies. Mr Jenkins retired from Brown's after twenty-three years and was succeeded by the first Lady Housemaster, Mrs G.L. Butler, now Lady Butler of Brockwell (note: *not* Housemistress). The following year Mr P.J.Gillard handed over Roper's to Mr M. Fosten and Mr D.W. Midgley handed over Spurgeon's to Mr E.M.D. Jones after twenty and four years respectively. In 1983 Mr G.R. McMillan handed over to Mr A. King after fourteen years as Housemaster of Dutton's.

In a mixed School personal relationships develop. Mr C.F.Liffen married Kate Hollingshead - one of the first four girls in the Sixth Form - who in 1992 was to become the first Old Girl President of The Edward Alleyn Club. Within the Common Room Mr E.M.D. Jones married Miss R. Sutton, and Miss E. McGann married Mr C.D. Chivers.

The year 1982 had arrived and Alleyn's planned to commemorate its first hundred years as a separate establishment within the College of God's Gift. On Founder's Day a copper beech was planted by Lord Wolfenden, Chairman of the Governors, to replace the beech that had stood at the side of the school since its erection but had been cut down because of old age. An avenue of trees was planted along the eastern edge of the Townley Field but, unfortunately, few have survived.

Centenary Commemoration Week was held in November 1982 when there was an Exhibition of Memorabilia loaned by Old Boys living not only in Britain but throughout the world. Many Old Boys returned to the School and over a thousand people in addition to the pupils visited the Exhibition. *The Magistrate* by Arthur Wing Pinero was performed for three nights in the Great Hall. The Edward Alleyn Club Dinner was held on the Friday evening with The Lord Archbishop of York presiding. On the following morning Speech Day took place with His Grace as the Guest of Honour and Mrs Stuart Blanch presenting the prizes. In the afternoon there was another entertainment in the Great Hall called *As Others See Us* with Prunella Scales and Timothy West (parents) and Julian Glover, AOB. Sunday was Remembrance Day when wreaths were laid on the War Memorial by the newly installed President of the Club, Tom Bamford, and the School Captain, Katherine McQuail, the first girl to hold the Office. The Sermon was preached by the Revd Michael Swindlehurst, AOB.

Centenary Speech Day   *Salmon*

Centenary Exhibition   *Salmon*

Planting the Centenary Tree   *Salmon*

The final event of Centenary Commemoration Week took place on Monday 15th November when a Choral and Orchestral Concert was held at Fairfield Hall, Croydon, before a large audience of Governors, parents and friends of the School. The Commemoration Coordinator was Arthur Chandler. This week of special events had brought together memories of pupils from the past and modern activities by pupils of the present, which augured well for the future.

To help this future, a Centenary Appeal, with the Archbishop of York as its Patron, was launched to raise £330,000 to pay for a new Technical Design Centre and a Field Study Centre with the added hope of raising additional money to build up a Bursary Fund for which there was an urgent need.

In November 1983 the Dulwich Picture Gallery served as the venue for the launch of the first printed and bound history of the School. Nearly two hundred people were present to hear Sir Colin Cole, Garter King of Arms, launch the book which was entitled *Alleyn's - The First Century*. The book was made possible by the kindness of Charles Skilton, AOB, a publisher who offered to underwrite the production of the School's history as his contribution to the Centenary Fund.

The target for this Fund was reached in December 1983 which enabled the Headmaster to proceed confidently with his plans for the new Technical Design Centre, a Field Centre near Buxton in Derbyshire and a larger Bursary Fund.

The year brought back memories of Harold Moody and Terence Higgins in past Olympic Teams when Zara Long aged 13 years was chosen to represent Great Britain in the swimming team that was sent to Los Angeles. She was the youngest girl ever to have been selected.

Air Marshal Sir Victor Groom, KCVO, KBE, CB, DFC, RAF
(Brown's, pre-1914)
The most decorated Old Boy, one of the senior guests at the Centenary

Tania Tribius as Leader of the Orchestra

Music Scholarships had been awarded annually by the School since 1977. These showed their worth now that Tania Tribius, the first Music Scholar, had become leader of the school orchestra and gave virtuoso performances of two violin concertos in her final year.

Fire destroyed the R.A.F. Hut and the glider but the disaster brought promises from the M.O.D. of replacements for both. It was also decided at this time that the CCF inspection would take place every two years rather than annually and would show training in action rather than concentrating on the ceremonial parade.

During the year another Common Room Wedding took place, this time between Mr J.C.F. Nash and Miss C.J.M. Peterson.

Speech Day in November 1984 was also a full Open Day showing many aspects of academic work. The idea of a double event had been growing over the years and had now come into fruition. The Guest Speaker was Julian Glover, AOB, with Lord Wolfenden in the chair. Unfortunately it was to be his last Speech Day as he died in January 1985.

He had been a remarkable Chairman of Governors strengthening the Foundation by guiding it with a strong and experienced hand through the early years of its first coeducational school. The Centenary Tree which he had planted will serve as a memorial to him for future generations. School and Old Boy representatives were present in Sanctuary for his Memorial Service in Westminster Abbey.

In the Summer of 1985 members of the CCF were to make their first parachute jump having been trained by the Red Devils who themselves landed on the Townley Field during the afternoon of Founder's Day. Three years after the first girl School Captain, the Corps was to witness, for the first time in its seventy years, the promotion of a girl, Elizabeth Chandler, to be the Senior Warrant Officer.

The opening of The Saddlers' Workshop as part of the new CDT Block took place on Founder's Day when visitors were able to see, in a tangible form, one of the results of the Centenary Appeal.

Two senior members of staff retired at the end of the school year: Gilbert McMillan, former Dutton's Housemaster and Head of Classics since 1963, and Colin Page, Housemaster of Cribb's. Cribb's was to become the second House with a Lady Housemaster when Mrs Gwyn Edwards was appointed to fill the vacancy.

By this time the Alleyn's Association had become a solid part of the Alleyn's family and, under the Chairmanship of John Parr, had forgotten its growing pains and could be relied upon to support the School in many ways. The Annual Jumble Sale came under the Social Sub-Committee of the Association and took place in the Old Gymnasium and on the Quad. It raised £5,000 each October for some years.

Sir Leonard Hooper, KCMG, CBE, AOB, became Chairman of the Governors of The College of God's Gift and was the first Alleyn Old Boy to hold the post. To do so he had to surrender the Chair of the Alleyn's School Committee. He was succeeded in this by Sir Douglas Henley, KCB.

Two generous bequests from Old Boys enabled the School to expedite the second object of the Centenary Appeal. A Railway Keeper's Cottage near Buxton became available for the School's Field Centre. A toilet and shower block were added to the Cottage and it was ready for visits by those training for the Duke of Edinburgh's Award and for visits by each of the First Forms towards the end of their first year.

Marking and preparation methods were beginning to change as staff and pupils prepared themselves for the new GCSE examinations starting in the summer of 1988. Although pressure on the staff was very high, they had mastered the transfer from one scheme to another in the same spirit as their predecessors had done forty years earlier when School Cert. became O Level and Higher Schools became A Level.

When girls entered the School, their uniform was virtually the same as the boys' but substituting grey skirts for grey trousers. In the summer term the girls had grey and white striped dresses. This was not to last for long and uniform regulations have in recent years altered much more frequently than in the past. In 1985 following a decision to allow Sixth Form girls to wear clothing 'appropriate to that worn by young ladies in City offices' it was decided that Sixth Form boys could wear suits but must continue to wear a school tie.

School Archives

When in 1981 Alleyn's was preparing for its Centenary Exhibition it was realised that the School had no Archives Collection. Our ancient history was deposited at Dulwich College and other records which had survived, mainly by luck, were in people's homes and a variety of rooms within the School. A request was made for archive material. Old Boys, widows and former masters donated items of historic value so that by the summer of 1986 the Collection which had been built up over the previous five years was gathered together in a 'temporary' Archives Room situated on the ground floor at the rear of the CDT Block. In order that this should have professional support, the Headmaster appointed Arthur Chandler as Honorary Consultant Archivist to the School and the Edward Alleyn Club.

In September the new Sports Hall, built alongside the swimming pool, was ready for use showing that the building extension plans of 1982 had made further progress. This addition to the School's facilities enabled the Alleyn's Association to launch a Sports Club for those in the local community as had already happened in our sibling schools. The building was officially opened on Founder's Day 1987 by Lady Wolfenden who named the building after her late husband.

Gill Butler

Senior staff changes started in April 1986 when Mrs Tessa Cox left to go to Liverpool where her husband had been appointed to the Chair of Psychiatry. She had been Senior Mistress since the introduction of girls. Mrs Gill Butler was appointed the new Senior Mistress and, in turn, her place as Lady Housemaster of Brown's was taken by Miss Sue Lane.

A major alteration in the administration of the Foundation came about with the retirement of David Banwell as Bursar and Clerk to the Governors for the previous twenty-five years. It was decided that both Alleyn's and Dulwich College should have their own Bursars, JAGS having had its own for the past few years. The new position of Clerk to the Governors would be the one coordinating factor in the whole Foundation including the Picture Gallery. Bob Alexander accepted this appointment while Michael Morley, Alleyn's Assistant Bursar, was duly promoted to the new post of Bursar within the School.

Girovend! This word entered Alleyn's vocabulary on the first day of Advent Term 1987 and soon became part of everyday life. The cashless society had arrived and the Headmaster decided that children must be trained for this. All the pupils were issued with plastic cards - not credit cards but cards that had a prepaid amount of money registered on them. There was now a cafeteria with a till at the end of the counter, not a money till but one that subtracted it electronically from the Girovend card.

Two Old Boys featured in the national news when Sir Philip Woodfield was appointed Ombudsman to the Civil Service and Sir Victor Pritchett was made a Companion of Literature by the Royal Society of Literature.

After nineteen years as Second Master, John Newton announced that he would retire in July 1988. He, instead of the Headmaster, gave the speech concerning the School at the Edward Alleyn Club Dinner in 1987. He had been an inspiration to many generations of boys and, more lately, girls. He guided the School through the interregnum before the arrival of Derek Fenner and also while the Headmaster was on sabbatical leave in Australia.

The Autumn of 1987 marked the Centenary of that memorable march through Dulwich Village when Joseph Henry Smith had led his boys to 'take possession' of the new building in Townley Road. Arthur Chandler had been installed as the Club's President at the Dinner mentioned above and it fell to him to deliver an illustrated lecture entitled *Sight and Sound* which told through slides and commentary the story of the School's main building since 1887. In addition to this special commemorative evening, two items were sold in aid of the School Bursary Fund: bone china plates depicting the 1918 drawing of the building tinted in water colour and numbered mounted prints of the original cover photograph for the School's history. Both were in limited editions of one hundred.

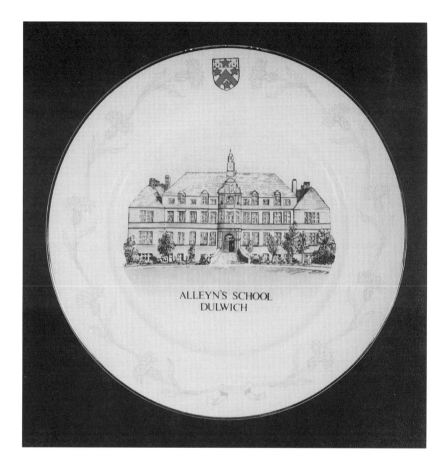

The Centenary Plate   *Ouzman*

By 1988 the number of staff had increased to over eighty. Some of the more senior, however, were due to depart. In addition to John Newton, Mr A King, Housemaster of Dutton's, left and was succeeded as Housemaster by Mr S E Smith. Jim Brew, Head of Art for the past fifteen years, retired. Other leavers included Derek Spedding, the Director of Music and The Revd Martin Oram who had been appointed Chaplain to the Parish of the English Community at Versailles.

Reg Hill, AOB, who had undertaken so much for the School's social and money raising activities, died during the year. As an Estates Governor and a former Club President he was greatly respected as was obvious at his funeral when the Foundation Chapel was full.

The School and Club were also sad to hear of the death of Sir Henry Cotton, AOB, 'golfer extraordinary', a few days before the publication of the Honours List where his name appeared.

The death of Dr 'Eddie' Giles, after eighteen years of retirement and twenty -eight years of teaching at the School, recalled a night during the Blitz when he was on firewatching duty. He was a Quaker and always undertook more than his fair share of firewatching and other 'non-combatant' duties. One evening he was patrolling the top corridor in the main building when an incendiary bomb fell into the gutter of the roof alongside him. It started to smoulder and the glow could be clearly seen. He reached into the gutter, took the bomb by its fins and carried it to the main corridor door nearest the fields. He threw it down and ran - within a few seconds the bomb went up in flames but only scorched the grass. His action had saved the building. Bravery was not in a Quaker's vocabulary. He had merely done what he should. His funeral was attended by the Head of English, the Library Master, staff members and numerous Old Boys headed by their President.

The window through which Eddie Giles climbed to grab the incendiary bomb

The Advent Term 1988 started without a 'Second Master' as the title of the second in command had been changed to Deputy Headmaster. The first person to hold this post was Peter Thompson who had previously been Head of the History Department at Portsmouth Grammar School. A new School Chaplain, the Revd Howard Jones, joined the staff. He was well over six feet tall and helped form an impressive trio on official occasions when standing with the Headmaster and the Foundation Chaplain who were also that height.

Neil Kinear, AOB, was appointed to the staff in September 1988 thereby filling the gap over the last six years for an Old Boy in the staffroom. The demands of the National Curriculum had now descended upon the School and the absorption of these new initiatives became a major task for the members of the Common Room.

The past was commemorated in November with a special W.J. Smith Centenary Concert at the Fairfield Halls in Croydon. It brought together pupils, parents and Old Boys in a fitting tribute to a man who was 'Alleyn's Music' for so many years. His *Music in Education* has remained a text book on how music can become part of school life and not be looked upon as an extra.

Alleyn's had become used to girls doing well within the School but it was felt that its new 'coeducation' was becoming known in other places when Madeleine Higgins, the School Captain in 1985, gained a Full Blue at Oxford in the modern pentathlon, the first Alleyn Old Girl to gain such an honour.

After eleven years as Foundation Chaplain, Canon Richard Lewis was appointed Dean of Wells Cathedral. He was a good friend to Alleyn's not only as a hard working Foundation Chaplain but also by gradually introducing the School into using the Church of St Barnabas.

Richard Lewis

Dora Wiggs, the first lady actually to be appointed to Alleyn's staff on a permanent basis, died on 6th October 1989 aged 90. She joined the Emergency School in London in 1943 and when the School returned from Rossall in 1945 she became a substantive member of the staff as a teacher of French. During the War she had worked for the French Resistance in London and also in France. Occasionally, at the beginning and end of terms, and possibly half-terms, she would be 'missing' for a few days. Teachers were as bewildered by her absences as the boys because she was such a hard working member of staff. Many years after the War she let slip about her activities in France as well as in London for the Resistance Movement. Her cycling everywhere in

Commander Tom Hodgkiss

London had obviously been carried on in France during her 'visits'. In 1951 she was decorated by the French Government and awarded the *Palmes Académiques* for distinguished service in the teaching of French. She was also decorated by General de Gaulle in 1946 for her services to the Free French.

As a teacher at Alleyn's she was described as "the best teacher in the School", "outstanding", "a fine colleague". The boys were worked extremely hard by her and every second of her lessons were of high powered instruction. Other teachers hated having to teach "the lesson after Miss Wiggs" as the pupils were so worn out. The School was her life, she helped in the library and assisted in many School plays. No boy took away bad memories of her when he left school. She retired to Eastbourne in 1967.

Tom Hodgkiss retired after a quarter of a century teaching Classics. It was he who introduced Classical Civilisation as a third subject within the department He had served as an Officer in the CCF for many years and was the Commanding Officer from 1982-1989 being the first, and so far only, Naval Officer to hold this post.

Perhaps, bearing in mind the profession of our Founder, it should be recorded that drama productions continue to play a dominant part in school life. During the year 1989-90 the following plays were performed: *The Doctor and the Devils, The Boundary Stone, The Lion in Winter, Candleford, Animal Farm, Softcops, The Laundry Girls,* and, needless to say, *The Sixth Form Revue!*

September 1990 started with 939 pupils, a record number for the school roll. Builders again moved on to the School site and it seemed that the ideas put forward in the recent Appeal would be able to bear fruit. The creation of a new Music School was started in the shell of the old brewery, built in 1899, which was to the north of the school boundary line behind the new sports hall. For the first time the School was going to build on ground that was not in the ancient Manor of Dulwich. To the north of the Music School was the Brooks and Walker building which Old Boys of earlier years will remember as the Jones and Higgins warehouse. Plans were now in being to demolish this and build a new junior school in its place.

Derek Fenner's last year at Alleyn's saw the opening of the Hooper Music School by Sir Robin Butler on Founder's Day. This was named after Sir Leonard Hooper, AOB, who chaired the Alleyn's School Committee for twelve years from 1947.

Old Boys who distinguish themselves seem to get younger every year, for Ajay Kakkar, who had been School Captain in 1981, became the youngest Fellow ever, at the age of 28, of the Royal College of Surgeons.

Two important staff departures at the end of the year were from the Mathematics Department. Iwan Davies left after twenty-two years service, eleven of those as Housemaster of Brading's. He revived the Gilbert and Sullivan era, taking a leading part in the many productions, and always sang in the School Choir.

Barry Banson

Barry Banson retired after thirty-four years on the staff, twenty-two of those as Housemaster of Tyson's. His last post in the School was that of Registrar. An incredibly sincere man who was an excellent teacher and marvellous with the children, he hated fuss of any kind and he just 'disappeared' after lunch on the last day of his last term without any farewells. Thankfully, he visits the School from time to time.

Duke of Edinburgh's Award

The time had come for Derek Fenner to retire. Under his guidance the School was producing real coeducation - not woodwork for boys and needlework for girls but absolute choice which enabled one to find boys in Home Economics and girls in Woodwork, all subjects were truly mixed. Pupils and staff were appointed for their ability: female house captains and female school captains appeared regularly.

The CCF became voluntary but alternatives included the Duke of Edinburgh's Award Scheme and various schemes for Community Service which included help in local schools and visits to the elderly. These activities were all part of the Fenner scheme for full participation in local and national life.

Outside the School he strove to given Alleyn's its rightful position within the Alleyn Foundation. He was instrumental in having the name changed from the Dulwich College Picture Gallery to the Dulwich Picture Gallery. He had Alleyn's share of the Chapel's seats increased for Foundation services and saw to it that the three took part jointly in Commemoration and Remembrance Services.

Outside the Foundation he was recognised as a pioneer in the transference of boys' Public Schools to mixed Public Schools. He served on the Headmasters' Conference Coeducation Group as Secretary for two years followed by a similar period as its Chairman. He was often called upon to be its spokesman.

It is interesting to note that for one of the years in which he held the Chairmanship of the Coeducation Group David Emms, Master of Dulwich College, was Chairman of the HMC and Bob Richardson, Headmaster of William Penn, was President of the NUT. The three leaders from the one Manor!

Derek Fenner had increased the school roll from 780 to 939, his enthusiasm and his faith that "it could be done" added many new buildings and much in-filling on campus. During the Centenary Celebrations in 1982, it was stated that Derek Fenner in seven years had formed a new school from the old. He then turned his attention to his vision of a Junior School which Alleyn's had not had since 1939. He became determined that such a school would be built during his Headship. In the next nine years the School blossomed forth into an example of modern education where results were good and the children were happy.

Alleyn's stood as a major part of the Foundation offering a service different from its sibling schools and standing in the forefront of Coeducational HMC Schools. The changes in society over the previous sixteen years had been reflected in the changes at Alleyn's School. The fact that these changes were both substantial and satisfactory were, in no small way, due to the dedication and leadership of Derek Fenner.

Hooper Music School

Mrs Bridget Weir, First Headmistress of the Junior School

ALLEYN'S JUNIOR SCHOOL
MRS B.M. WEIR, 1992–

DEREK FENNER'S VISION came into reality when the Junior School building was growing daily during the last year of his headship and he, in conjunction with his successor Dr Colin Niven, was able to appoint the first Headmistress to work on campus during his last term.

Mrs Bridget Weir arrived at Alleyn's in April 1992 from being head of the Junior Department at St Hilary's School, Sevenoaks. There was no school building that she could enter and therefore the Headmistress-elect and her secretary camped out in a spare room in the new Music School. She had, however, been in from time to time and, assisted by wives of Alleyn's staff and friends of the School, was able to test and interview children for entry. These tests and interviews were undertaken in January and February for entry to a then non-existent building. Not only Mrs Weir but also the parents had a great deal of faith that everything would be ready on time. The first Deputy Head of the School was Mrs Jennifer Strong who had just had great experience as Acting Head of JAPS and knew Alleyn's already through her children who were educated at the Senior School.

For the first time since September 1938, Junior School entrants arrived at Alleyn's gates on the 10th September 1992. One of the Headmistress's comments echoed the tones of the Headmaster of the School over fifty years before when she said that the school was "A place where the children matter first and foremost as individuals".

One hundred and thirty-three new pupils, ten new staff and one brand new building, that had only been completed four weeks before, came together to form a new school of children from five to ten years of age.

In November 1992 Terry Waite, the Archbishop's envoy who had recently been released after some years as a hostage in the Middle East, was Guest of Honour at the Senior School Speech Day. After the morning's ceremonies he officially opened the Junior School which now had 173 pupils.

Simon Ward

It was hard to believe that the school had only been in existence for fourteen months. There were four Houses (Jaguars, Leopards, Panthers and Tigers) fully established. Inter-school sports activities and dramatic productions were becoming established. A Junior School Parents Association had been started and was being very supportive to school activities in general. Not only were children and staff learning about the history and traditions of Alleyn's but they were making history and starting traditions as the new school took shape.

The 375th Anniversary of the Alleyn Foundation had a great effect on the life of the Junior School during the year 1994-1995 as not only was it the ideal year in which to learn about the past but the Junior School was to act as host to the *Alleyn Foundation Pageant* to be held in the School grounds in May 1995. The Pageant covered the history of the Manor of Dulwich and the Alleyn Foundation from 1127 to the present day. There were nine cameos, three each performed by pupils of James Allen's Preparatory School, Dulwich College Junior School and Alleyn's Junior School. An orchestra of musicians from the three schools was trained and conducted by Ms Jo Brooke. Over four hundred pupils performed the pageant before an audience of more than twelve hundred parents and friends.

The Pageant was devised and directed by Arthur R Chandler, AOB, assisted by Mrs Angela Rossetti, a senior school parent. The narration, bringing the cameos together, was delivered by the actor Simon Ward, AOB.

The culmination of the Anniversary Year was the visit to the Junior School by Mrs Eileen Carey, wife of the Archbishop of Canterbury. The Archbishop is Visitor to the Foundation and his wife asked to see the Junior School at work while he was visiting the Senior School.

The new Junior School came under inspection by the Incorporated Association of Preparatory Schools early in its life and was admitted to membership of the IAPS in September 1994.

By now the traditions of the Junior School were well established. Plays and musical events appeared regularly in the calendar. School journeys both at home and abroad were accepted as part of the normal activities. Inter school sport was taking place nearly every week. The Parents Association had established its own type of Founder's Day working in cooperation with the Senior Association and The Edward Alleyn Club to make this century old commemoration a friendly and family day.

Alleyn's Junior School Building

Anniversary Pageant, ready to perform

Junior Jazz Band

The Junior School prospectus clearly states that Alleyn's Junior School is a Christian School of an Anglican Foundation and that daily assembly for the whole school includes worship. There is a termly service for the Juniors in the Foundation Chapel with that in the Trinity Term being held on or near 21st June.

Since 1882 until the present day, with the exception of the years 1982-1988 there has always been at least one Old Boy on the staff of Alleyn's. It is most appropriate that this tradition should be carried on in the Junior School with the appointment in 1996 of Miss Kate Foley, AOG, to the Junior School staff.

Cricket is exceptionally strong. The Under 9s team of 1995 were unbeaten as the Under 10s and Under 11s. This is due in no small way to the inspiration given to the boys by Mr Das Gupta. Swimming is also very strong, in 1996-97 the School winning seven of its eight matches. In the same year the Netball Team came thirty-sixth out of ninety schools in the IAPS Under 11 tournament and came third in the local tournament at Bromley where twenty schools took part.

It is obvious that the pupils enjoy their school activites and put a lot of energy into all that they do both in the classroom and in the sports arena. Energy is also diverted to help others and support is never lacking for charitable causes. The effort put into raising £1,000 for CRISIS from the sale of cakes and cards and into collecting £749 in pennies for Red Nose Day was tremendous.

Junior School Magazine

School work must not be forgotten as the 11+ entrance examination is usually the goal of most parents. In a typical year all Year Six Leavers pass the entrance exam to the School of their choice, 70% of these obtain places in the Senior School at Alleyn's having passed the entrance exam, as there is no 'automatic entry'. One quarter of the children win scholarships not only to Alleyn's but to other schools. These Scholarships are not only academic but are often in music or art.

Success of a School often causes casualties in the Senior Administration. It was proved that Alleyn's Junior School had really grown up when Jenny Strong the Deputy Headmistress was appointed Headmistress of Hornsby House, Balham, to take over in September 1998. She had been a very influential pillar of the establishment in the building process of the new School and she had seen children who had entered in the first year go right through the School to leave in year six. Her successor is Miss Catherine Mitchell from Ashville College, Harrogate.

Last year the School had a letter from a man who had been a schoolboy at Alleyn's for ten years (1934-43), three of them in the pre-war Junior School, which took boys from eight years old. He proudly wrote "Junior School and Tulley's" after his name. Within a few years current pupils will be signing themselves in a similar way.

Albert Spring, the Headmaster of the old Junior School from 1909 until the war started in 1939, when it ceased to take boys under eleven, would have been very proud of the present pupils and staff, they have assumed the Alleyn's mantle and are wearing it well.

ALLEYN'S JUNIOR SCHOOL – SCHOOL CAPTAINS

1992-1993	Toby Arul-Pragasam
1993-1994	Laurie Booker
1994-1995	Camilla Taylor
1995-1996	Tom Matthews
1996-1997	Natalie Shur
1997-1998	Louisa Hill
1998-1999	Frelder Camm
1999-2000	

Dr Colin Niven   *Liffen*

Dr C.H.R. NIVEN, 1992–

DR COLIN NIVEN was appointed Headmaster during Derek Fenner's last year and for the first time in thirty years there was a smooth and direct handover from one Headmaster to another.

This arrival was really the case of a boy coming home (but deciding to live in the house nearby). As a five year old young Colin had been dragged to the Village Infants School by his mother and for four months there was a tug-of-war between the Headmistress and his mother on one side and him on the other. He cried every day but, after four months, he thought better of it and has never left school since. He moved from the Infants to Dulwich Hamlet and then to Dulwich College where he was to become School Captain. He went up to Gonville and Caius, Cambridge, and thus becomes the third Headmaster of Alleyn's from that seat of learning. His Dip.Ed. was taken at Brasenose College, Oxford and his Doctorate comes from the University of Lille in France. He then taught at Fettes and Sherborne. He has been a member of the Headmasters' Conference for some years having been Headmaster of the Island School, Hong Kong and St George's English School in Rome.

Unlike most new appointments he did not need a year to settle in upon his arrival back in Dulwich. He already knew the local shops. He knew the area, the School's traditions, where the Chapel was and how to be a headmaster.

After his interview by the Governors it was suggested that he went for a walk or visited the Art Gallery while they made their decision. Soon after his arrival at the Art Gallery, the School Serjeant appeared and addressed him as "Mr Headmaster". He then knew that he had returned to the Foundation.

Lt Colonel A.S. Jenkins, AOB

The first official engagement outside the School for the new Headmaster was to attend the Memorial Service in the Foundation Chapel for Stephen Jenkins. He had an incredible school record. He entered Alleyn's as a pupil in 1932 and became a School Prefect in 1938. He joined Alleyn's Staff after leaving Cambridge in 1945 and was immediately commissioned in the School Corps. He served under four Headmasters and was Head of Drama from 1964 for ten years. He was Housemaster of Brown's from 1968 until 1981 and Commanding Officer of the CCF from 1974 until his retirement from the School due to ill health in 1982. He enjoyed ten years of retirement in Cambridgeshire where he died in July 1992. The

Chapel was full of Old Boys, parents and friends with the CCF providing a Guard of Honour.

The guest of honour at Dr Niven's first Speech Day was Terry Waite who not only spoke and gave away the prizes but then officially opened the new Junior School. The new Head set about introducing his personal ideas when he introduced the 'Headmaster's Book' for outstanding achievement and the issue of a monthly newsletter to all the parents. He was writing one of these on the day that he could see from his windows the smouldering ruins of St Barnabas Church which was burnt down during the early hours of the morning of 2nd December 1992.

Leavers during this year included many who have had a great effect upon the life of the School. John Clarke joined Alleyn's in 1961. Eight years after his arrival he was appointed both of Head of Science and Housemaster of Bradings. During his time he organised the internal examinations and also the internal 'eblephone' system. Throughout his thirty-two years at Alleyn's his meticulous brain contributed greatly to the records of School life.

Colin Rouse had been at Alleyn's for 28 years and in that time he had only two days sick leave. His influence on Alleyn's has been widespread. He was on the Admissions Committee. He ran cricket teams, he took pupils on Fell walking holidays and was Housemaster of Tulley's for 22 years. He was Master-in-Charge of the Grounds and the trees for twenty years. His greatest asset as a Schoolmaster was his personality and he was able to put all of this into development of the Field Centre from its inception.

David Midgley came to the School in 1964. He was Head of the CDT Department and examples of his personal work could be found in the construction of special 'props' for school plays. One of his main interests was the RAF Section of the CCF where he served as an officer for 24 years. He often served as a Lower School Form Master thereby putting the youngsters on the right road for the rest of their school life. He served as Housemaster of Spurgeon's from 1978-82.

Other long serving staff were John Courtney who had served for 37 years. He was very much a backroom boy and was responsible for the 'white book' which listed all the achievements of pupils and took hours of research to find all the information required in time for Speech Day.

Born in 1926, Eric Randall joined the Grenadier Guards in which regiment he became a Gold Sergeant before his eighteenth birthday. When he was demobbed in 1947 he was appointed the contingent RSM to Alleyn's School JTC. He then thought that he might take the job for a few months until he had settled into civilian life. The few months became 46 years.

Major Hudson, then Headmaster, saw not only the military potential but also the civilian administrative potential of this young man. He brought him into School life in general and appointed him to the ancient office of School Serjeant. He came to school seven days a week - the School then worked on Saturdays and he came in on Sundays to deal with the stores. The JTC soon became the Combined Cadet Force and his School role as major-domo of all exams and functions gradually evolved. The Head would tell Mr Randall what function was to take place and Mr Randall would then create the 'system'. Outside the School he was involved in the formation of the National Youth Theatre as he had acted as controller for the crowd scenes in Michael Croft's production of *Julius Caesar* when the Army cadets were on one side in the play and RAF were on the other. He helped with the Summer vacation productions and was called back to deal with the Prussian Army in the twentieth anniversary production at the NYT. He has arrested intruders including an Old Boy trying to force an entry into the Science Block. During the headship of Charles Lloyd he stopped a truck fly-tipping in the School grounds and suffered a badly broken leg in so doing. After the lorry incident he and his family moved into Hillsborough Lodge in the grounds. His two sons David and Andrew both came to Alleyn's and both subsequently entered the Services.

In 1988, forty years after he joined the School, The Edward Alleyn Club held a special evening Reception to honour Eric Randall. For his services to the School and the Club, he was created an Honorary Alleyn Old Boy and presented with a special certificate to commemorate this. That particular evening had a group of men over fifty years old thanking Eric for the help he had given them thirty-five years earlier.

He was normally very welcoming but knew also how to dispose of people, especially Lower School parents who brought their offspring on the first day of Advent Term. On 4th July 1993 *This is Your Life Eric Randall*, compered by David Weston, AOB, was presented when three Headmasters, former staff and generations of AOBs and AOGs assembled in the Great Hall. The event was attended by over 300 people representing all years from 1947 to 1993. Many who could not be present sent recorded video messages that were played during the presentation. A Guard of Honour was provided by serving officers from the three Services who had been cadets under Eric. Particularly impressive was the revelation that during his years nearly 6,000 pupils passed through his hands. On 3rd August he was gazetted Major in the *London Gazette*. His spirit still remains in the School because his bronze bust sculpted by Helen Chown stands on a plinth in the entrance hall "In grateful appreciation of loyal and devoted service to the School from 1948-1993 the longest period by any individual in the history of Alleyn's College of God's Gift".

In 1993 Sir Victor Pritchett AOB had been created a Companion of

Honour, in 1994 Professor R.V. Jones AOB received the same honour. Two great AOBs died this year: Sir Lennard Hooper (Roper's 1926-34) was one of the first to benefit from the Sixth Form introduced by R.B.Henderson. In 1938 he joined the Government Code and Cipher Section at Bletchley where he was appointed Director GCHQ in 1965. As already stated he was first Chairman of Alleyn's School Committee. His memory is kept alive as the new Music School was named after him.

The Rt Revd and Rt Hon The Lord Blanch of Bishopsthorpe (Stuart Blanch, Brown's 1929-36) died in 1994. He was a choir boy at Holy Trinity Church, Trinity Rise and during his period at Alleyn's helped to build the running track on the upper field. He left School to become an insurance clerk but joined the RAF in 1940. During his War service in the Far East he underwent an evangelical conversion and after training was ordained in Oxford Cathedral. After various academic and ecclesiastical appointments he became Bishop of Liverpool in 1966. He was called to be Archbishop of York in 1979 and then became a member of the Privy Council. His memorial service was held at York Minster, when the School and the Club were represented.

In 1992 whilst making notes before one of the numerous meetings that a headmaster has to attend, Colin Niven realised that the Foundation was getting near its 375th Anniversary. In March 1993 he called together a meeting of the Master of the College, the Headmistress of JAGS, the Foundation Chaplain, the Director of the Picture Gallery, the Clerk to the Governors and the Archivists of the School and the College. It was agreed that the 375th Anniversary of the Foundation should be celebrated over the year from June 1994 until June 1995. It was further agreed that Alleyn's School should coordinate the events and that Arthur Chandler should be invited to be the Honorary Coordinator. The Anniversary opened on Sunday 19th June when the Revd Canon David Keene AOB of Southwell Cathedral preached a sermon. This was followed by a Commemoration Garden party in the grounds of JAGS.

Departures and reorganisation within many departments led to new appointments. Ladies had been on the staff for many years but now their presence was to take another step forward and create another milestone in the School's history with the appointment of the first lady Head of Department when Miss Wendy Collins took over as Head of Chemistry.

Retirements during the year included David Johnson who came straight from University in 1959 and spent all his 35 teaching years at Alleyn's, the past twenty-five as Headmaster of the Lower School. He was firm and kind and children always felt that they could go to him with their personal problems. He taught both History and Latin. He was succeeded as Headmaster of the Lower School by Steven Smith.

Mike Salmon left upon his appointment as Head of Science and Technology at Surbiton High School. He came to Alleyn's in 1978 straight from Imperial College. His many contributions to the School included great drama productions. *Anne of Green Gables* and *My Fair Lady* with the Derby Day scene in the original costumes were memorable.

Wendy Collins, Head of Chemistry, with leavers 1996

The 375th Anniversary continued into the next academic year with plays by the Schools, a lecture on Marlowe in the Old Library of the College and a special exhibition: *Edward Alleyn, Actor and Collector* at the Picture Gallery. On Remembrance Sunday, Derek Fenner, former Headmaster, being then President of the Edward Alleyn Club laid the wreath at the War Memorial and the sermon was given by The Very Revd Dr Wesley Carr, OA, Dean of Bristol and Chairman of the Chapel Committee.

Souvenirs were on sale throughout the three schools in order to help defray the costs of this special year. These included 375 special bone china mugs which sold out very quickly. In addition to the usual souvenirs of pens, key rings and tea towels, there was a cornflower blue tie with the personal shield of Alleyn upon it. This has proved to be well received and is intended to be worn by persons from all parts of the Foundation

The design of The Edward Alleyn Mug shows our Founder and is based on an original line drawing made in the 1930s for the front cover of *The Edward Alleyn Magazine.*

The outdoor spectacular was in May when the Pageant described in the chapter on the Junior School was performed in Alleyn's grounds.

The greatest day of the 375th Commemoration Year was the visit of the Archbishop of Canterbury who was welcomed to the Foundation on the Headmaster's lawn and then toured parts of the School before visiting our sibling schools and also the Foundation Chapel where Lower Sixth representatives from the three Schools assembled to ask him questions. While Dr Carey visited the main building and the CDT Department, Mrs Carey visited the Junior School.

A highlight of the Anniversary Year was a concert by the most talented instrumentalists of the three Foundation schools at St John Smith's Square - the first time that the three schools had combined for their music making. Not only was the standard extremely high but it obviously created a precedent because combined concerts have been held annually ever since.

For two years Sir Robin Butler had headed a commission to look into the running of the Alleyn Foundation, how the income should be shared and how it should be governed. The plan, details of which are given in the chapter on The Dulwich Estate, came into being on 1st August 1995. The Art Gallery took its share of Foundation money and with a substantial grant from outside made itself completely independent. Alleyn's and Dulwich College for the very first time were to have two different Boards of Governors. Alleyn's therefore had to say goodbye to Sir Colin Cole, a former Garter King of Arms, as he would no longer be the Chairman of our Governors. This position was taken up by Ronnie Gray who had been Chairman of the Alleyn's School Committee at the beginning of the Advent Term 1995.

The Archbishop with the School Captain, Ben Woodd

Alleyn's School Board of Governors

Standing (left to right): Michael Morley (Bursar), Admiral Sir Michael Boyce, Peter Thompson (Deputy Headmaster), Lord Higgins, AOB, Professor 'Jeremy' Cowan, Raymond Cousins, AOB, (Chairman, Development Committee), Bridget Weir (Headmistress, Junior School), Colin Niven (Headmaster), Campbell Pulley, Bob Alexander (Clerk); seated (left to right): Gordon Mackay, Professor Winifred Watkins, Ronnie Gray (Chairman), Angela Horne, AOG, Peter Glossop (Chairman, Finance Committee), Joyce Baird. Absent: Kate Jenkins.

No likeness of H.Baker had been known until a photograph of him and his staff was found behind a cupboard at Dulwich College. This enabled photographic portraits of five of the former Headmasters to be added to the portraits already hanging in the Great Hall. On Founder's Day these portraits were unveiled accompanied by a dialogue on the history of these men which had been written by Mrs Lesley Morris, a parent at the School. Charles Lloyd was present to unveil himself!

The history of Edward Alleyn and 'God's Gift' had been told earlier in the day in the Founder's Day sermon delivered that year by Arthur Chandler, AOB, a rare honour for a layman.

In June 1995 nearly forty Alleyn Old Boys returned to Rossall for two days in order to commemorate their stay on the spartan north-eastern coast some fifty years earlier. The oldest of the group was probably Ken Spring who went up to Rossall with his father who was then Headmaster of the Junior School. Ken took with him pictures that he had painted in the early forties before he left for War Service which included a period in the Far East. Jack Lanchbery and Donald Leinster-McKay had both travelled from Australia for the Reunion.

Upon arrival at the School, the AOBs were taken on a tour of the buildings to see the various changes that had taken place. Like Alleyn's, Rossall has progressed to coeducation and in the year of the visit was opening up for day pupils.

An afternoon of Cricket was followed by the Reunion Dinner in the Masters Dining Room. Speakers included the current Headmasters of both Alleyn's and Rossall (by far the youngest participants on parade) and the Edward Alleyn Club President, Peter Reeve, who had started Alleyn's School life in Lancashire.

The following morning all the visitors attended the School Chapel Service during which a wreath was laid jointly by the senior officer present from both schools. The group photograph shown here was taken before School lunch in the dining hall, after which the Old Boys gradually left to return to the latter part of this century and their memories.

The retirement of Alan Berry after twenty four years service at the School was marked on 14th July with a gathering of sixteen football teams and over two hundred players to participate in a unique soccer tournament tribute for all that he had done for the hundreds of boys he had coached through the years.

Another departure was that of Philip Meaden who after fourteen years in the Music Department, eight of which as Director of Music, left upon his appointment as Academic Director of the Trinity College of Music. His influence on School music will last for many years to come.

Two untimely deaths hit the School in 1996. Steven Pearce, the School Technician of extreme ability, who was married with a young son, died of cancer. Christian Berglund, an Old Boy in his early twenties and a brilliant cricketer died unexpectedly of a sudden illness.

Two time capsules were buried during 1996. The pupils placed one under the Globe Theatre on Bankside and members of The Edward Alleyn Lodge encased another behind the Foundation stone in the new St. Barnabas Church.

St Barnabas Time Capsule

Reunion at Rossall, June 1995

Alleyn's never had a copy of the Grant of Arms made to the Foundation in 1936 when, to make the School different from the College, Henderson used 'God's Gift' as the motto under the Shield. In 1993 Sir Colin Cole as Garter King of Arms kindly had a special copy made of this Shield 'as displayed by Alleyn's School'. This painting, authorised by Sir Colin, now hangs in the Entrance Hall of the School.

A major School Inspection took place early in the Advent Term 1995. Thirteen Inspectors, many of them Heads of famous schools, spent a week not only sitting in on lessons but also meeting parents, former pupils and governors. The inspection team concluded that Alleyn's was 'a very good school with an unusually high number of teachers rated good to outstanding'. The Daily Telegraph chose our Inspection Report as one of the best in the country.

Headmasters and their architects seem, in many cases, to be able to add considerably more space for school needs without taking up any more ground. The old staff dining room was pulled down and the patio outside it was dug up - this allowed for a very spacious Staff Dining Room, staff toilet facilities and a new serving counter. At the other end of the pupils' dining room a large toilet block was added.

In the summer holiday of 1992 the Library had been refurbished and upon his arrival Dr Niven named it 'The Fenner Library'. In 1997 this facility moved further forward with the installation of ever improving methods of Information Technology. Underneath the Library, the Old Buttery was completely cleared and in its place a new Sixth Form Centre including its own refreshment facilities was built.

The General Election in May 1997 led to the withdrawal of Assisted Places from 1998, and the elevation of Sir Terence Higgins to a Life Barony in the Dissolution Honours List. He had already decided to retire from the House of Commons where he had held the Office of Financial Secretary to the Treasury in a previous administration. Well known as a runner whilst at school, he was a member of the British Athletics Team in the 1950s. He has been a School Governor for some years and is a former President of the Edward Alleyn Club.

Lord Higgins is the third AOB to be so honoured. E.H. Lamb who entered the School in 1891 was also a Member of Parliament and was created a Baron in 1931 with the title of Lord Rochester. Archbishop Blanch also received a Life Peerage upon his retirement as Archbishop of York.

Two famous Old Boys died during the year, Sir Victor Pritchett, the author, who gave the School the handwritten text of the first two pages of his autobiography *Cab at the Door*, and Sir Ronald Leach, a former President of the Club, who was described in St Paul's Cathedral at his memorial service as 'the greatest British accountant of this or any other country'.

A tree planting ceremony took place before lunch on Founder's Day 1997 to commemorate the lives of Steven Pearce, and Eileen Chivers who, soon after she left Alleyn's, became a victim of cancer and died in December 1996.

The School was presented with 'the Interim Standards Organisation 2009 Quality Award for Catering', the first School Caterers to be so honoured.

The Rt Hon, The Lord Higgins, KBE,DL
Terence Higgins (Dutton's) 1942–46   *Universal Pictorial Press & Agency Ltd, EC1*

The New St Barnabas Church   *The Revd Richard Cattley*

At the end of term Gill Butler retired from the staff. She was the first Lady Housemaster (Brown's), then became Senior Mistress and finally a Second Deputy Head. She had already retired from these posts to teach part-time in order to support her husband Sir Robin Butler in his official duties as Secretary to the Cabinet. In January 1998 Sir Robin was elevated to the Peerage upon his retirement and with his new title, Lord Butler of Brockwell, is now Master of University College, Oxford.

The week after the School's return for the Advent Term 1997, the death was announced of Derek Fenner, the previous Headmaster, from leukaemia. Staff and pupils were shocked by his early death. The School flag flew at half mast for a week and his name was engraved on the memorial panel in the Foundation Chapel before the day of his burial in Cornwall.

A memorial service conducted by The Revd Richard Cattley, Chaplain to the Foundation and the Revd Howard Jones, School Chaplain, was held on 6th November 1997 at St Barnabas Church where a moving address was given by Martin Fosten.

Representatives of the Foundation, HMC Schools, his Cricket Club and his friends joined members of the School, past and present, in a fitting tribute to a great Headmaster.

The basement of the main building has been used throughout the years for many purposes. It was originally built for servants' quarters (residential), a boiler house and a very large store for coal (for form room fires) and coke (for hot water). At the same period there was a large staff changing room and staff toilet. Servants quarters gave way to a Billiard Room and a School Shop. The fuel store was bricked in to provide a Prefects' Room and a Sixth Form Common Room. Part of the old inner fuel store was turned into stores for the CCF whilst a room on the front part of the building was turned into the Officers' Mess. The change of use for the basement, now called the 'lower ground floor' has been constant so it was no surprise to find that it was again to be transformed, this time to become the Maths Department. Old Boys will be very surprised to find a complete carpeted area with brilliant lighting rather than the concrete floors and dimness of the days of storage or the Wartime days of the corridor acting as an air raid shelter.

Michael Morley who had been School Bursar since 1987 and an Assistant Bursar for the ten previous years retired from his post at half term. At the Edward Alleyn Club Dinner he was made an Honorary Old Boy for his work on behalf of the Club and the School. On the right he is seen with his daughter, Penny, who was School Captain in 1986. Her year in office was the last in which the prefectorial blazers were worn.

Mike Morley was succeeded by Terry Mawhinney who had just completed his Commissioned Service in the Royal Engineers at Chatham.

Amongst the many prizes awarded each year is the Eric Randall Travelling Scholarship which is awarded to the pupil in the Lower Sixth who gives the best reasons for 'travelling with a purpose'. The 1997 Award went to Davide Lees who travelled through Italy making a tour of the Churches. He was a brilliant pupil and obtained one of the highest A Level results on record. He has now entered a seminary in the Vatican to test his vocation for the Catholic Priesthood.

Eric Randall's successor, Paul Lambert, was a Warrant Officer in the Devon and Dorset Regiment and now holds the joint post of RSM to the CCF, and School Serjeant. He has fully upheld the traditions he inherited.

Davide Lees on the Randall Scholarship, 1997

Mike and Penny Morley

CCF Mascot, 1997

On Remembrance Sunday 1997 the three Schools had representatives in the Guard of Honour for the first time as four girls from JAGS had joined Alleyn's CCF.

The picture shows the Corps' mascot with the Goat Major wearing the sash previously worn by Ken Farrington when he was Drum Major. The Goat's ceremonial coat was specially made to match the Drum Major's sash. The Officer with the bugle is John Lofthouse who joined the staff in 1996 already having an interesting connection as he is an Old Rossallian. He also takes his Common Room membership of the Edward Alleyn Club seriously as he appears in their Drama productions.

History has shown that in coeducational schools marriages are likely to occur between members of staff. This can be straightforward but when some ladies keep their maiden name for work within the school it can lead to 'interesting' questions. Mike Salmon married Dr Julia Warwick, both on the staff. Some time afterward, two rather worried first year girls told a master that they thought that Dr Warwick was having a baby and (sotto voce because they did not know they were married) "we think Mr Salmon is probably the father"!

Following a precedent set by the Liffens, Mike McCaffrey became engaged to Suzie Jones soon after she had left the Sixth Form. They married two years later in 1996. Anna Hamburger and Richard Halladay both from the Common Room married in 1997 thereby becoming the fifth couple

Needless to say, Chris and Kate Liffen's two sons are being educated at Alleyn's, the elder, James, was appointed one of the Vice Captains of the School for the year 1998-99.

With marriages one looks forward and with retirements one looks back. The end of the Trinity Term 1998 was the appointed time for Bob Alexander to retire from the post of Clerk to the Governors. He had succeeded David Banwell who had been extremely helpful in the original negotiations for the introduction of both coeducation and the Saddlers' Scholarships to Alleyn's. Bob Alexander's place in the School's history is no less, as it was he who worked with Sir Robin Butler on the introduction of the changes within the Foundation that took effect on 1st August 1995. The School owes Bob a great debt for all efforts to create an amicable situation within which the new allocation of resources could work. He is succeeded by John H Jackson to the joint post of Clerk to the two separate Governing Bodies of Alleyn's School and Dulwich College.

A New Wing in the North East Quad, 1998

Schools appreciate high powered Clerks and Bursars but they also appreciate hard working and dedicated Schoolkeepers. This was shown at Mid term in the summer of 1998 when David Eburne retired from Townley Lodge. Townley Lodge is a modern bungalow built in the early 1960s on the site of the original Porter's Lodge built sixty years earlier when the 'school servants' ceased to live in the basement of the main School building. The most memorable of the occupants of that Lodge was 'Stevens', his Christian name was definitely not known by the boys and probably not known by most of the staff. In his navy blue uniform with brass buttons, he would patrol the corridors looking through the doors to see that the fires were burning well and that the young boy servants, younger than most boys in the School, had put on sufficient coal. He would enter each form room every morning to put the names of absentees in his book and on Friday afternoon would arrive to read out the names of those who would be required to stay for Saturday afternoon detention after the normal session of Saturday morning school.

One of the most interesting visits during Dr Niven's Headship was that by Edward Upward who was a fellow writer with Isherwood and a contemporary of Auden. He taught at Alleyn's from 1932 to 1961. Allison appointed him as the first Head of English at the School in 1942. Until then it had been taken for granted that all form masters taught their own form English! During his visit he met one of his old pupils - who in 1948 was the first boy to take English as a main subject in the Sixth Form.

An Alleyn's boy during Upward's time is now the local Old Boy Author, Brian Green who, this year, is publishing a book *Ten Walks Around Dulwich* to add to the three books he has already written on Dulwich and *To Read and Sew*, a history of JAGS, published in 1991.

Half way through Derek Fenner's term of office he entertained a prominent Old Boy to lunch and was asked by him "what happens to the Girls, do they all become secretaries and nurses?" "No" replied the Head, "they become doctors and solicitors".

The Old Boy actors of the Michael Croft era have now been joined by those more recent Leavers such as Sam West and Jude Law. In the modern vein, Ed Simons, otherwise known as the Chemical Brothers, is also a former pupil.

As was seen on the previous page changes in the School buildings are still taking place with the quadrangle being gradually closed in. In the pipeline are ideas for a new pavilion and even a School theatre. Whether these will come soon or take as long as the Junior School, time alone will tell.

The coeducational school has produced, in addition to the normal run of AOBs into the professions, an AOG School Governor, Angela Horne, an AOG Inspecting Officer for the CCF Inspection, Major Emma Peters (née Gillespie), AOG barristers, doctors, musicians, solicitors and teachers. On 28th June 1998 Maria Reeves became the first Alleyn Old Girl to be ordained into the Church of England thereby following in the footsteps of the Old Boys who have accepted the same calling.

Within the School the only distinction between boys and girls seems to be in the allocation of changing rooms and certain games, otherwise, to quote Gilbert and Sullivan "all shall equal be".

Alleyn's School provides real coeducation in a happy atmosphere. Behind it all is the Headmaster's steady hand pushing towards the double goal of good academic results and sound preparation of every child for facing the future in the adult world.

The Revd Maria Reeves, AOG
(Roper's 1989–91)

Edward Alleyn House (Almshouses)

Dulwich Estate Offices

*Dulwich Estate
Coat of Arms*

Raymond Cousins, AOB
Chairman of Dulwich Trustees, 1997 and 1998

THE DULWICH ESTATE

THE DULWICH ESTATE is the new title given in 1995 to the body previously known as the Estates Governors of Alleyn's College of God's Gift.

The Charity Commission Scheme of 31st July 1995 tidied up and modernised the Foundation Charities as they were administered during the previous century. These Charities were:

1. The Charity called Alleyn's College of God's Gift (Educational) regulated by 23 different schemes or amendments the earliest dating back to 4th June 1913 and the latest dated 28th October 1994.
2. The Charity called the Eleemosynary Branch of Alleyn's College of God's Gift at Dulwich regulated by the Endowed Schools Act of 18th August 1882 and altered by ten different Schemes or amendments dating from 1891 to 1983.
3. The Charity called the Chapel Endowment of Alleyn's College of God's Gift at Dulwich regulated in the same way as (2) above.

New titles for the above Charities from 1st August 1995 are:

1. The Dulwich Estate
2. The Dulwich Almshouse Charity
3. Christ's Chapel of God's Gift at Dulwich

Part of the investments of Charity (1) were transferred or paid as follows:

a) St Olave's and St Saviours Grammar School Foundation £559,873
b) The Central Foundation Schools of London £1,882,850
c) James Allen's Girls' School £4,290,480
d) Dulwich College £6,065,850
e) Alleyn's School £4,438,427

The remainder of the investments continue to form part of the permanent endowment of Charity (1).

Some land and buildings were also apportioned to Dulwich College and Alleyn's School. In effect these were already accepted as being part of, or belonging to, the two schools.

Within the 1995 Scheme of the Charity Commissioners there are nine Interpretations of titles of individual Charities. Seven are obvious but two could usefully be recorded here:

> "The Dulwich Schools" means the College, Alleyn's and JAGS
> "The Beneficiary Charities" means St Olave's, Central Foundation, the Dulwich Schools, the Almshouse Charity and the Chapel.

A Board of Trustees was appointed for The Dulwich Estate consisting of 14 competent persons 11 of whom shall be nominated as follows:

> One each by the Lord Archbishop of Canterbury, the President of the Royal Institution of Chartered Surveyors, the Governors of St Olave's, the Trustees of the Central Foundation and the Trustees of the Almshouse Charity.
> Two each by the individual Boards of Governors of the College, Alleyn's and JAGS.

153

The Board Room, Dulwich Estate Office   *Ouzman*

An Original Fireplace,   *Ouzman*
Dulwich Estate Office

John Wylie
General Mananger and Secretary

Although members of the first Board were appointed for periods ranging from two to five years, in future all Trustees will be appointed for a period of five years and may be appointed for a further five year term. They may not however be appointed for a third term.

The Trustees' duties include the Management, Letting and Disposition of land. Application of the Income from The Dulwich Estate is laid down as follows:

a) Yearly a sum not exceeding £80,000 to the Trustees of the Almshouse Charity

b) Yearly a sum not exceeding £30,000 for the purposes of the Chapel

c) The remainder of the Estate's income to be allocated:

    i) 3.248 % to St Olave's

    ii) 10.923 % to the Central Foundation

    iii) 85.820 % to be divided between the Dulwich Schools in proportion to the average number of pupils in each school during the preceding three years.

The Charity Commissioners on 31st July 1995 also laid out a Scheme for the appointment of separate Boards of Governors for the three Dulwich Schools. Each should have a Board consisting of not less than ten and not more than fourteen competent persons. In the case of the Alleyn's Board it is stipulated that one of the Governors should be nominated by The Worshipful Company of Saddlers.

The term of office for a Governor of the Dulwich Schools is the same as for the Dulwich Trustees (see above). There is also an age bar as no person may be appointed a governor who will reach the age of 75 years during his/her term of office. The administration of the Estate is under the control of The General Manager and Secretary who is responsible to the Board of Trustees. The present incumbent is John Wylie who worked in collaboration with the Clerks and

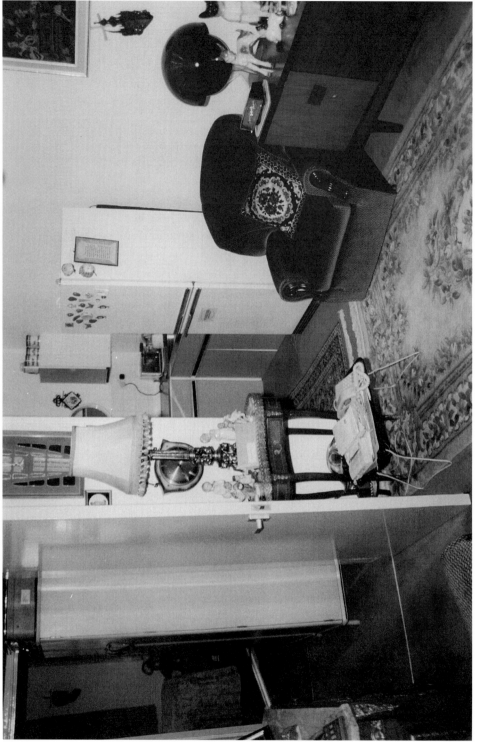

Inside one of the Almshouses

Chairmen of the Board   *Ouzman*

representatives of the other boards on the 'Butler Commission'. Without the strong efforts of John Wylie, Bob Alexander and John Reed and the great guidance of Sir Robin Butler, the 1995 Scheme for the Foundation would never have materialised. Dulwich and all the beneficiaries will benefit from their wise decisions for many years to come.

Not all the former beneficiaries remained within the Alleyn Foundation to share in the Scheme of 1995. The Trustees of The Dulwich Picture Gallery agreed to a financial arrangement whereby they were given a capital sum in March 1994 and surrendered all future claims on the Charity. In reality they have become financially independent but work amicably with all parts of the Foundation. Similarly the St Luke's Parochial Trust withdrew, after the payment of a capital sum, in October 1994.

The Chairman of the Estate Trustees for 1997 and 1998 is Raymond Cousins who was an Estates Governor and appointed to the first Board of Trustees. This is the first time that an Alleyn Old Boy has held the office.

CHRIST'S CHAPEL
OF ALLEYN'S COLLEGE OF GOD'S GIFT
AT DULWICH

CHRIST'S CHAPEL of Alleyn's College of God's Gift at Dulwich is the full title of the Foundation Chapel which serves not only the three Foundation Schools but also the residents of the Almshouses (later Edward Alleyn House) and other inhabitants of Dulwich who wish to worship within its walls.

On 17th May, 1613, Edward Alleyn signed a contract with John Benson, bricklayer of Westminster, for the building of his College, the central part of which was to be the Chapel. It took three years to build. On 31st August, 1616, The Revd Cornelius Lymer, Chaplain of Christ Church, Oxford, was appointed as Chaplain and on the following day, Sunday 1st September (the Founder's fiftieth birthday) the Chapel was consecrated by George Abbot, Archbishop of Canterbury who, on the same day, consecrated the Burial Ground at the other end of the Village. The many distinguished visitors on that day included The Lord Chancellor, Francis Bacon, who three years later on 21st June, 1619, was to issue the Letters Patent, on behalf of King James I & VI to Edward Alleyn, officially to enable him to create The College of God's Gift. The Archbishop of Canterbury became The Visitor to the Foundation, a post held by all his successors albeit that today the post is an honorary one.

In 1634 Archbishop Laud, as Visitor, admonished the Master, Warden and Fellows "that thereafter they doe daily weare their surplices . . . there duly to attend divine service . . . as well on Sundays as other dayes, and that the Bason and two candlesticks which the Master confesseth hee tooke away from the altar and keepeth att his chamber in the said Colledge be placed there againe".

In 1638 the steeple of the Chapel, then on the south side, fell down and all the College buildings were in need of repair. The financial situation was so bad that the Archbishop closed the College for six months from 10th October, the revenue thus saved helping considerably towards the cost of repairs. The construction of the building was weak for in 1656 it was again badly in need of repair and five years later part of it collapsed. This time the Master, Thomas Alleyn, a cousin of the Founder, came to the rescue by lending money for the repairs.

Gilbert Sheldon became Archbishop of Canterbury in 1663 and was shocked to find that a detachment of soldiers from Fairfax's army had been quartered at the Chapel and had "committed great havoc". During the Commonwealth the Organ, built by Gibbs of Powles in 1618, was broken up and carried away, the staff and boys were forbidden to wear surplices, the Communion Table was turned end ways East and West and 'several other disorders had crept in'. The Archbishop commanded that these things be done as formerly and that a Reading Desk for the lessons, a Litany Desk and a small Organ be provided that they might have their service in the Chapel "according to the statute as near to Cathedrall fashion as may be". A new Organ was built in 1669 by Bernard Smith.

Christ's Chapel looking West

Ouzman

In October, 1706, The Revd James Hume of Edinburgh was appointed to the Schoolmaster Fellowship of the Foundation. He was largely responsible for putting the Foundation on a sound financial footing and remained a Fellow for twenty-two years. He was author of the Latin inscription over the porch at the Chapel entrance which, in translation, concludes "Blessed is he who takes pity on the poor, go thou and do likewise". In front of the Vestry door can be seen Hume's gift to the Chapel: a cream marble Font with a copper cover around which is a Greek palindrome commanding, in translation, "Wash away sin, not the visage only".

In 1751 it was decided that £20 per annum should be set aside towards the cost of a replacement Organ. Eight years later George England and Thomas Whyatt were asked to build a new Organ in the Chapel to be played for the first time on the last Sunday in August 1760. The present Organ includes what is believed to be the earliest surviving work of George England and stands in the carved case with the ornamental pipework built in 1760. The curious reversal of the colours of the key-board has been retained. It was restored in 1888 and reconstructed twenty years later. An electric blower was installed by J. H. Gauss in 1931. An inspection and renovation was undertaken by N. P. Mander in 1969.

On the North wall of the Chapel are two important paintings. The copy of Raphael's 'Transfiguration' was painted by Julio Romano, one of his talented pupils, and was presented to the Chapel in 1769 by Thomas Mills who purchased it from Christie's Auction Rooms for £60. It was originally used as an Altar-piece. The copy of Raphael's 'Ansidei Madonna' was executed by Ethel Galer, a Dulwich resident.

In 1816 a Turret Clock was placed in the North Tower of the College. It was ordered that it was "to go for eight days and to strike the quarters". In the same year a new black marble slab was placed over the Founder's Tomb. The old stone was discarded but found some years later in the yard of The Half Moon from which it was, thankfully, retrieved and now stands in the North Cloister.

By 1822 the population of Dulwich had outgrown the seating capacity of the Chapel which then only covered the area of the Chancel, the seats from there to beneath the organ gallery and the few seats in the organ gallery. Substantial alterations were called for. In 1823 the South Wall of the Chapel was demolished and pillars with arches put in its place to support the roof. A complete new South Aisle was added at ground level and a new gallery, the length of the Chapel, covered the South Aisle. This increased the capacity from about two hundred to over five hundred.

In the early 1850s an Oak Screen, Pulpit and carved pews were added to the Chancel to enhance the setting for the Founder's Tomb. New congregational pews were added to other parts in 1891.

The next major change took place in July 1911 when the present Reredos, created by W. D. Caroe, was dedicated to the memory of Canon A. J. Carver, the first Master of the newly created Dulwich College (i.e. not The College of God's Gift). The two side panels of the Reredos depict the Annunciation of the Blessed Virgin Mary.

The central panel depicts the Epiphany. One of the Kings is dressed in

Centre of the Reredos   *Banwell*

seventeenth century robes, the two boy attendants are in the costume worn by the first Scholars at the College. One holds a model of the Chapel, the other holds a cornflower which is traditionally the Founder's favourite flower and is worn by members of the Foundation on Founder's Day and Commemoration Sunday. The Gold Cup offered by one of the Kings is copied from a silver gilt chalice of 1599 which is still used in the Chapel for Holy Communion at High Festivals.

On either side of the Reredos are oak panels inscribed with the names of the sixteen Masters of the College of God's Gift including the first Master of Dulwich College to whom this memorial is dedicated.

On the North Wall of the Sanctuary are recorded the names of the Masters of Dulwich College, the Headmasters of Alleyn's School and the Headmistresses of James Allen's Girls' School who have departed this life. To the visitor, it must be pointed out that their names are inscribed in order of their demise, not in order of their service.

Towards the end of the nineteenth century the population of Dulwich increased rapidly. Fifty years after the additions to the Chapel it was not big enough for the congregation wishing to attend and although a new Parish of St Paul's, Herne Hill, was formed in 1868 such provision served only the fringe areas of the Dulwich Estates. The Estates Governors therefore provided ground for a new Church and Vicarage for a newly created Parish of Dulwich. The Church was dedicated to St Barnabas and situated in Calton Avenue. It was consecrated on 11th June 1894 but was destroyed by fire on 2nd December 1992. A new St Barnabas Church with a unique glass spire was opened in September 1996.

The many Old Alleynians and Alleyn Old Boys who were killed in the Great War of 1914-1918 are remembered on the panels that were erected on the South Wall of the Chapel beneath the gallery and were dedicated in 1920.

Other memorials erected between the two wars include the Baptistry panelling in memory of William Clifton, an Estates Governor who died in 1925, the Bishop's Chair in memory of John Ratcliffe Cousins, a College and Estates Governor who died in 1928 and the Cloister entrances erected in 1935 in memory of Richard James May, J.P., and his wife.

In 1943 the Chaplain's House was destroyed by a bomb and the Chapel was badly damaged. Services continued in the Old Grammar School while temporary repairs were carried out. It continued in use, despite further blast damage when the Art Gallery was bombed, until 1950 when it was closed for permanent repairs and for the installation of a new heating system. It was re-dedicated by the Lord Bishop of Southwark, Bertram Simpson, AOB, on 28th September, 1952.

In 1954 the Bishop returned to dedicate a new East Window which depicts, in the lower left-hand light, a figure of St Nicholas of Myra and in the lower right-hand section, Edward Alleyn at prayer with an old man and an old woman symbolising the Almspeople, with the Old College in the background. The upper right-hand light is symbolic of Charity while the upper left-hand symbolises the Faith of the Church. The Coats-of-Arms of the Foundation and the Diocese, flanked by Alpha and Omega, are seen at the top while the centre light depicts the Blessed Trinity.

The most recent glass, by Carter Shapland, is on the North Wall of the Nave and shows the instruments of the Passion. It is in memory of H. F. Bromfield, who died in 1968, and his son A. F. Bromfield, who was killed in action in Burma in 1952. On the same wall, a window displays St George and St Augustine and was given in 1952 in memory of J. M. Galer and his wife, Louisa Jane.

The only pre-war glass to be seen in the Chapel is in the East Wall at floor and gallery levels.

In October 1976 the Chapel was closed for reordering and restoration. The main changes were the provision of a free-standing Altar to meet the current liturgical requirements and the lowering of the solid panels in the Screen so that the congregation had a better view of those in the Chancel. Modern lighting was also installed. It was re-opened on 23rd January 1977 in the presence of the Bishop of Dorking, an OA, and the Bishop of Woolwich.

It was decided in 1957 to have the same person holding the posts of Vicar of Dulwich and Chaplain to the Foundation. The Revd Canon Wilfred Brown held the two posts as a temporary measure in the latter years of war and continued as such in the early years of peace seeing through the rebuilding of the Chapel after its bomb damage but relinquishing the Foundation Chaplaincy upon its restoration. The Revd Canon Arthur Perry, AOB, was the first person to hold the joint living permanently and was installed in 1957. He was succeeded in the Autumn Term of 1979 by The Revd Canon Richard Lewis who, upon his appointment as Dean of Wells, was followed by The Revd Richard Cattley in 1990. In addition to the Foundation Chaplain there are now individual Chaplains to both Dulwich College and Alleyn's School.

In the centre of the pathway between the gates and the Chapel entrance stands the War Memorial to members of the Foundation who gave their lives in the two World Wars. On Remembrance Sunday each year wreaths are laid by the President of the Edward Alleyn Club and by the Captains of the three Dulwich Foundation Schools. This ceremony is followed by a joint service in the Chapel.

The three Schools use the Chapel for various services throughout the academic year but the only other occasion when they officially worship together is on Commemoration Day which used to be the Sunday nearest 21st June upon which date in 1619 James I & VI granted Letters Patent to Edward Alleyn thereby creating The College of God's Gift. This Commemoration has recently been transferred to the last Sunday in the Trinity Term which will usually, but not always, fall on the first Sunday in July.

THE FOUNDER'S PRAYER
(used at all services within the Chapel)
We give Thee humble and hearty thanks, O most merciful Father, for the memory in this place of Edward Alleyn, our Founder and Benefactor, by whose benefit this whole College of God's Gift is brought up to godliness and good learning: and we beseech Thee to give us grace to use these Thy blessings to the glory of Thy Holy Name, that we may here fulfil the good intent of our Founder, and become faithful servants to Thee and to our country; and at last be made partakers in Thy heavenly promise of the life everlasting; through Jesus Christ or Lord. Amen

THE EDWARD ALLEYN CLUB

THE Alleyn Old Boys' Club sported an Annual Card, and it stated thereon that the Club was formed on 18th April, 1884. How is it then that the Club celebrated its Jubilee in 1932 and its Centenary in 1982?

Until the 1880s the number of Old Boys from the Lower College of God's Gift was very small and an Association seemed hardly possible. There was sufficient support in 1877 to form a Cricket Club and in 1882 an effort was made to form a Social Club. It took shape as a Geological Club. It visited the South Kensington Science Museum and held discussions on rocks, volcanoes and "the nature and composition of the earth's interior". The Revd J.H. Smith suggested that the members of this Club and any other Old Boys might like to pay an annual subscription and have an Annual Dinner on a definite date. This was received with enthusiasm and a meeting was organised for 19th March 1884 to discuss the idea. It was agreed and the Foundation Meeting of the Edward Alleyn Club was then held the following month. The seed, however, had been sown with the Geological Club two years earlier.

On 17th January, 1906, the title of the Club was changed to the "Alleyn Old Boys' Club" which was used until November, 1977, when it reverted to its original title, due to the arrival of "Old Girls" in an "Old Boys'" Club.

The President's Badge of Office, here seen on Tom Bamford, President 1982-3, was presented to the Club at the Annual Dinner in 1937 by the President for that year, Howard Foulds. He was Secretary of the firm of Callenders' Cables but he was also one of the last Foundation Scholars and he can be seen in the uniform of 1883 in the photograph on page 22. 1985 saw the amalgamation of the old Athletic Club with the central Club thereby making them one which had been the aim of many of its members for many years past. Sir Cyril Pickard was the first President under the new Constitution and John Jewson became the Club's first Chairman. The control of the Club then came under a Council of elected members and representatives of the various sporting sections.

In 1985 the first of the revived House Reunion Dinners was held when past pupils of Brown's House together with the current House Prefects assembled on the evening before Founder's Day. The idea of House Reunions was then accepted for an eight year cycle that would always be held on the Friday evening before Founder's Day: 1986 Tulley's, 1987 Spurgeon's, 1988 Brading's, 1989 Dutton's, 1990 Cribb's, with Roper's in 1991 and Tyson's in 1992.

At Burbage Road, the old tennis court area that had not been used for twelve years was developed in 1986/87 into a new multi sports surface which not only has allowed the Edward Alleyn Tennis Club to rise again and a new Netball section to be formed but enabled the Club to welcome the School as users from time to time.

The present Clubhouse is a replacement for the one that was destroyed by fire many years ago. Rebuilding on the same site was not then completed as sufficient funds were not available. Thanks to Sir Lindsay Alexander, President 1986/87, a rebuilding scheme was set up and an Appeal was organised by Peter Reeve, the Club's Secretary. This action helped raise the money required by obtaining income from special events and donations from friends. Additions to the building took place in 1989 and provided extra rooms, a kitchen and refurbished facilities.

A brooch showing the school crest on a gold bar was introduced for Old Girls in 1983 and AOGs have been on the Club's Council ever since. The first Lady Officer of the Club was Kate Liffen (née Hollingshead) who became Editor of the magazine in the summer of 1986 and first Lady President in November 1992.

Membership of the Club has grown rapidly since the middle of Derek Fenner's Headship. It was he who masterminded the scheme whereby the Life Subscription to The Edward Alleyn Club was included in the last year's fees at the School. This not only brought in an annual income to the Club but also provided it with an address list with which to make contact in the years immediately after leaving School. In this way contact is made with the non-sports members and those living away from Dulwich on a much firmer basis than before.

The Clubhouse in Burbage Road is now nearing the end of its first decade, the Appeal of eleven years ago has more than proved its worth. Not only is the Clubhouse considerably larger but substantial refurbishment has brought the older parts of the building up-to-date. It acts as a centre point of contact for at least seven different groups. The Alleyn Old Boys' Football Club has its home ground in Burbage Road as does the Alleyn Old Boys' Cricket Club. These have a continuity of action that can be traced for over a century. The definitive School Cricket Records dating back to 1890 have just been collated by two Old Boys, Richard Godfrey and Tom Harris, and are proving extremely useful as a reference document. The Edward Alleyn Tennis Club was rejuvenated when the new Pavilion was opened and has prospered ever since. Three Hockey Clubs also use the Pavilion for social activities: The Edward Alleyn Hockey Club, The Dulwich Women's Hockey Club and The Dulwich Hockey Club. All these titles on a recently installed board at the entrance to the grounds display the varied use of both Clubhouse and grounds.

The most interesting daytime use of the Clubhouse is that by 'Little Fingers Montessori Nursery' which is a Registered Nursery School for children from $2^1/_2$ to 5 years old. This is proving of great value to the local community where there are waiting lists for all the nursery schools.

Although matches are obviously played elsewhere, The Edward Alleyn Golf Society is very active as an individual sports section within the Club.

The New Clubhouse, Burbage Road

Membership of The Edward Alleyn Club is automatically granted to all former pupils of the School and all members of the Common Room. This means that all members of one family can be members of the Club. The first family to qualify was the Chandlers in 1994, the next was the Godwins in 1998 and then will follow the Liffens and the Jones family over the next eight years. After that it will probably become commonplace as both parents of pupils could well have been pupils themselves.

The Club not only provides the Sidney Incledon Scholarship, which enables a pupil of limited means to remain for the Sixth Form, but also sponsors some leavers in their gap year in order that they have the funds to undertake Voluntary Service Overseas.

The President's Badge of Office presented to the Club in 1937 had the words 'Alleyn Old Boys Club' surrounding the shield. John Pretlove, President 1996-97, decided that the President should have insignia with 'Edward Alleyn Club' around the shield and kindly presented the Club with this new piece of regalia which was first used at the Installation of Timothy Inge as President in November 1997.

When the Club took over The *Edward Alleyn Magazine* in 1969, it became a white fronted Magazine with the title at the top of the front page. In 1982 it reverted to the blue cover with the figure of Edward Alleyn, striding through the Village, on the front. Under the editorship of David Hankin the form of the magazine took a bold step forward in May 1991 to become an A4 glossy magazine with blue as well as black print and photographs strategically inserted to support the text. This well produced magazine has a circulation of over two thousand copies world wide. Its correspondence section has encouraged some of the backwoodsmen to come forward with their memories.

John Pretlove, Raymond Cousins and Peter Reeve

Representatives of the Club always attend both Commemoration Day and Remembrance Sunday Services in the Foundation Chapel. The picture above shows three of our senior members on Remembrance Sunday 1997.

The Edward Alleyn Lodge has been holding its Lodges of Instruction in the main School since 1983 thereby returning to pre-war practice when Tulley and Tyson controlled these meeting as an extension of the classroom. When the Lodge was looking for a new place in which to hold its regular meetings in 1993, it was fortuitous that the newly built Junior School welcomed the Lodge to hold its meetings in the Reception Hall. Membership of the Lodge, which is increasing annually, has staff members and parents as well as Old Boys.

In September 1996 the Lodge celebrated its 75th Birthday under the Mastership of David Johnson when a Banner was presented to the Lodge by Sir Colin Cole former Chairman of Governors and former Garter King of Arms. Wives and non-Masonic guests attended a floral display at the same time and then all joined together in the Junior School Hall for a birthday dinner for one hundred people.

For the first time since the fifties, Drama again became part of the Club's activities. A monthly play reading circle, under the leadership of Angela Horne, developed into an acting group called 'The Burbage Theatre Company'. Its first production was *Mixed Doubles* in November 1997 and was followed by a full length play *Whodunnit?* in May 1998. Both evenings were presented at the School in the Old Gym which the group transforms into a very presentable theatre.

Although there have been lady officers over the last twelve years, the Club has a little further to go than the School in equality for its lady members. However, good progress is being made.

EDWARD ALLEYN CLUB PRESIDENTS

1884-1900	The Rev J.H. Smith		1957	C. W. Burman
1901	F.A. Mayne		1958	Leslie W. Farrow, CBE
1902	C.F. Redman		1959	J. Nye
1903	A.J. Roper		1960	The Rt Rev Bertram Simpson, MC, Bishop of Southwark
1904-05	W.J. Woolrich			
1906	F. Collins		1961	Richard Lydall
1907	J. Attfield		1962	A.H. Mann
1908	F.A. Mayne		1963	S.R. Hudson
1909	A.E. Watts		1964	Z.T. Claro, MVO, OBE
1910	W.J. Woolrich		1965	Air Marshal Sir Walter Pretty, KBE,CB
1911	G.E.J. Swift			
1912	A.J. Hudson		1966	S.R. Incledon
1913	W.W. Russell		1967	Prof R.V. Jones, CB, CBE, FRS
1914	S.A. Hill		1968	Cecil Addington
1915-19	A.E. Watts		1969	R.G.R. Wall, CBE
1920	C. Isaac		1970	Vivian Frank, FCA
1921	H.L. Hough		1971	Dr Gordon Watts, CBE
1922	S.J. Brading		1972	C.R. Allison
1923	J.A. Nye		1973	R.G.D. Vernon, MBE
1924	H.W. White		1974	Sir Leonard Hooper, KCMG
1925	W.J. Fitter		1975	J. Somerville
1926	L.W. Brown		1976	Sir Frank Young, CMG
1927	F.H. Holland		1977	Philip Hall
1928	S.H. Carter		1978	Sir Ronald Leach, GBE
1929	C. Petherbridge		1979	Charles Lloyd, JP
1930	W.J. Woolrich		1980	James Maple
1931	H.L. Hough		1981	The Most Rev & Rt Hon Dr Stuart Blanch, Archbishop of York
1932	W. Penman			
1933	J.V.H. Coates		1982	Tom Bamford
1934	C.H.J. Day		1983	John Jewson
1935	H. Reynolds		1984	Sir Cyril Pickard, KCMG
1936	H. Foulds		1985	Dennis Lomas
1937	S.H. Payne		1986	Sir Lindsay Alexander, JP
1938	G.H. Clark		1987	Arthur R. Chandler
1939-46	A.F. Day		1988	Rt Hon The Lord Higgins, KBE,DL
1947	C.S. Herridge		1989	Alun Williams
1948	E.C. Robbins		1990	Raymond Cousins
1949	A. Spring		1991	Micky Stewart, MBE
1950	The Rt Revd W.H.Bradfield, Bishop of Bath and Wells		1992	Mrs Kate Liffen
			1993	Derek Fenner
1951	T.T. Nye		1994	Peter J. Reeve
1952	Maj. Gen. Sir Leslie Hamlyn Williams, KBE, CB, MC		1995	Dr Michael Sneary
			1996	John Pretlove
1953	W.S. Arnold		1997	Timothy Inge
1954	H.L. Rouse, CBE		1998	
1955	R. W. Hill		1999	
1956	Sir Cullum Welch, Bt., Lord Mayor		2000	

HEADMASTERS OF ALLEYN'S

1882-1902
The Revd J. H. Smith

1902-1903
H. B. Baker

1903-1920
F. Collins

1920-1940
R. B. Henderson

1940-1945
C. R. Allison

1945-1963
S. R. Hudson

1963-1966
C. W. Lloyd`

1967-1975
J. L. Fanner

1976-1992
D. A. Fenner

1992-
Dr C. H. R. Niven

Headmasters of the Lower School
of the College of God's Gift

1858-1870
Dr W.F. Greenfield
1870-1875
The Revd B.C. Huntley
1875-1882
The Revd J.H. Smith

Headmasters at SLESS at Alleyn's
(During the Second World War)

1940-1943
C.E. Hack
1944-1945
C.F. Tyson

SECOND MASTERS

S. J. Brading	1882-1922
A. E. Cribb	1922-1925
A. J. Skinner	1925-1929
J. V. H. Coates, AOB	1929-1933
R. L. Taylor	1933-1944
S. R. Hudson	1944-1945
C. F. Tyson	1945-1947
L. H. Jones, AOB	1945-1951
S. Incledon	1951-1969
J. W. Newton	1969-1988

DEPUTY HEADMASTERS

P. C. Thompson	1988-

SENIOR MISTRESSES

Mrs Tessa Cox	1975-1987
Mrs Gill Butler	1987-1988

SECOND DEPUTY HEADS

C L Liffen	1988-
Mrs Gill Butler	1988-1990
Mrs Ilze Termanis	1988-

HOUSEMASTERS

BRADING'S

S J Brading	1907-1922
H Gregory	1922-1945
F M Goldner, AOB	1945-1969
J S Clarke	1969-1980
I P Davies	1980-1991
A M Bruni	1991-

BROWN'S

E C Brown	1907-1925
R L Taylor	1925-1944
B E G Davies	1944-1947
F A Meerendonk	1947
L A R Shackleton	1947-1967
A S Jenkins, AOB	1967-1980
Mrs G L Butler	1980-1987
Miss S A Lane	1987-

CRIBB'S

A E Cribb	1907-1925
W R Morgan	1925-1936
L H Jones, AOB	1936-1951
M H Cocks	1951-1957
R R S Barker	1957-1977
C Page	1977-1985
Mrs G Edwards	1985-1990
G Tonkin	1990-1995
R G Halladay	1995-

DUTTON'S

F Dutton	1921-1923
C E Hack	1923-1944
S Incledon	1945-1969
G R McMillan	1969-1983
A King	1983-1987
S E Smith	1988-1994
Miss S P Chandler	1994-

ROPER'S

A J Roper	1907-1918
F Linnell	1918-1927
F A Rudd	1927-1944
W J Smith	1944-1948
E F Upward	1948-1961
P J Gillard	1962-1982
M Fosten	1983-

SPURGEON'S

J F Spurgeon	1907-1909
C L W Kingswell	1909-1928
Sir John Maitland, Bt.	1928-1949
G E Dodd	1949-1955
G R Charnley	1955-1958
W M S Boyd	1958-1970
E Marsh	1970-1972
M E Shepherd	1972-1978
D W Midgley	1978-1982
E M D Jones	1982-

TULLEY'S

S J S Tulley	1907-1925
J V H Coates, AOB	1925-1933
Sir Rodney Paisley, Bt	1933-1936
S R Hudson	1936-1945
R H D Young	1945-1971
C A Rouse	1971-1993
P R Sherlock	1993-

TYSON'S

C F Tyson	1921-1947
J A Taylor	1947-1948
E F LeFeuvre	1948-1949
J Logan	1949-1968
B Banson	1968-1990
Mrs J M Helm	1990-1998
Mrs R A Thomson	1998-

STAFF LIST

Several documents relating to the period 1882-1913 have been studied in order to compile the first part of this list. From 1913 to 1958 a Register of Staff was kept fairly diligently. The Register was started by F. Collins, then the Headmaster, who entered the existing staff according to some order of seniority. Therefore the entries from S.J. Brading down to J.F. Spurgeon are not in date order. The order in the Register, which extends to W.H.N. James, departs from date order on a few other occasions for reasons unknown.

The list since 1958 has been compiled from a few typewritten sheets found in the back of the Register, from the School Magazine and from the Annual Roll. The Magazine, however, has said farewell to some staff who were never welcomed and welcomed others who were never bade adieu.

B G Jenkins	1867-1889	W R Morgan	1906-1936
L C Nightingale	1879-1904	J Williams	1907-1937
W Raybould	1885-1900	F A Rudd	1907-1944
C Stanton	1893-1907	C L W Kingswell	1903-1928
W H Ault	1898-1906	F Dutton	1904-1923
Revd A H Knott	pre 1900-1903	R L Taylor	1906-1944
W F Smith	pre 1900-1901	E F P Carrick	1887-1923
J J Pilley	pre 1900-1902	E Reydams	1899-1917
F C Weedon	pre 1900-1903	L Hirsch	1899-1918
J R Phillips	1900-1905	H Gregory	1907-1944
R G Wilson	1900-1903	W Hutt	1907-1944
- Andrews	1900	H H Finch	1904-1928
C B Gutteridge	1902-1905	J Davis	1904-1912
L K Hindmarsh	1902-1903	W Wintersgill	1906-1922
F G Hargan	1903	J F Spurgeon	1904-1909
Stevenson	1904	C H Pritt	1909
R G Telfer	1906	C E Hack	1909-1944
H Carter	pre 1912	A Spring	1909-1949
Revd W E Catlow	pre 1912	W E Weber	1909
S J Brading	1881-1922	C W G Livermore	1910
A J Roper	1872-1918	J A Imison	1911
J H Marsland	1878-1919	H J Millar	1911
F G Cross	1888-1915	C F Tyson	1911-1947
A E Cribb	1889-1925	G Eaton	1912
C N Riches	1889-1920	W G Heal	1912-1944
S J S Tulley	1894-1925	J H Knight-Adkin	1913
F Linnell	1897-1927	L H Jones, AOB	1914-1951
A F Callaghan	1900-1929	C H W Martin	1914-1919
J V H Coates, AOB	1900-1933	A Dimmer	1915
A J Skinner	1900-1929	J J MacGinley	1915
A Geeson	1903-1911	P G Bestall	1916
P W A Cooke	1903-1939	V R Duigan	1916
E C Eayrs, AOB	1905-1945	N G Evans	1916-1943
E C Brown	1906-1925	F E Skinner-Jones	1916

H J Williams	1916-1946	S R Hudson (*see Headmasters*)		1926-1945
E T Griffiths	1916-1917	E N Parker		1926
F D Wray	1917-1920	H M Wright		1926-1949
	& 1923-1924	C E Young		1927-1929
A E P Voules	1917	H R C Carr		1927-1931
A R Cowman	1917-1918	J Mansbridge		1927-1928
H G Benner	1917-1919	M S Gotch		1926-1928
P C Binns	1917-1925		&	1932-1935
C L Derryer	1917	R O Gartside-Bagnall		1928-1930
G E Dodd	1917-1955	W H Carter		1928
W J Woodruff	1917-1918	G A Hutchings		1928
E O Donnell	1918	T W H Holland		1928
W O Trivett	1918-1919	V K Haslam		1928-1955
H C Cooksey	1918-1919	B C M Dixon		1928-1931
	& 1920-1925	J H G Pell		1928-1939
H B Hayley	1918	A S H Mills		1929
	& 1919-1925	S Incledon		1928-1969
C Hirst	1918-1919	J S Shields		1928-1934
P W Norris	1920-1949	A G Gooch		1929-1935
Sir John Maitland, Bt	1920-1949	R McGregor		1929
H V Alker	1920-1922	A L Hutchinson		1929-1931
W E C Browne	1920-1921	C J McClymont		1929-1953
Revd M P Shipman	1920	R M Bentham		1929
H Dixon	1920-1924	J M Hegarty		1930-1931
L Soar	1920	B E G Davies		1930-1947
H P Snowden	1921-1954	R L W Jones		1930-1941
J F E Monckton	1921-1927	G A W Denny		1930-1931
Sir Rodney Pasley, Bt	1921-1925	G J Ososki		1931
	& 1931-1936	A C P Payne		1931
E F Welek	1923-1932	W O Bell		1931
M Williams	1923	E L Franklin		1931-1945
H V Anson	1923-1924	M G Crewe		1931-1970
A Bolton	1923-1925	J W Gray		1931-1936
	& 1928-1930	J F Doubleday		1931-1945
H C Whaite	1924-1929	J W Horseman		1932-1935
F T S Dyer	1924-1928	E F Upward		1932-1961
W R Watkin	1924-1928	A H Waters		1932-1965
F M Bannister	1924-1928	F M Goldner AOB		1932-1965
K G Burns	1924	Miss E H Young, *Librarian*		1932-1939
W J Smith	1925-1948	J A Taylor		1934-1948
L V Ottaway	1925	F A Meerendonk		1935-1947
W H E Stevens	1925-1931	R H D Young		1935-1971
C E Wallis	1925-1926	E N Eccott		1935-1946
G A Brown	1925-1935	F LeFeuvre		1936-1949
G L Heawood	1925-1929	F Holliday		1936
A H Parker	1925-1927	A L Bickford-Smith		1936-1947
M G G Hyder	1925-1932	A W A Spicer		1936-1937
E J J Somerset	1925-1930	A A Fletcher- Jones		1937

Name	Dates	Name	Dates
A R B Fuller	1937	T E Evans	1954-1982
M C Green	1937-1947	R E Groves	1954-1961
L A R Shackleton	1937-1967	D L Metzger	1954-1958
C T A Hankey	1941	C C Allsopp	1955-1959
G U Whitehead	1944	S J Edgoose	1955-1959
J F Galleymore	1944-1947	P J Gillard	1955-1988
C H Williams *SLESS 1942*	1944-1957	D J Morton	1955-1963
Revd C W Ayerst	1944	N T Poulter	1955-1959
J Lanchbery AOB	1944-1945	A E Aston	1956-1968
J R A Bottomley	1945	R J Courtney	1956-1993
D H B Pritchard *SLESS 1943*	1945-1969	Revd P G Medd	1958-1971
H I T Rees *SLESS 1943-*	1945-1967	W H N James	1957-1961
J Logan *SLESS 1943*	1945-1968	D W Muffet	1957-1961
M H Cocks	1945-1957	T B O'Hara	1957-1961
J M Cohen	1945	R C Abbott	1958-1966
Miss D E Wiggs *SLESS 1942*	1945-1967	B Banson	1958-1992
A S Jenkins AOB	1945-1983	D A Raeburn	1958-1962
E L Giles *SLESS 1942-*	1945-1970	P W Sumsion	1959
Miss T J Ratzer *SLESS 1943-*	1945-1947	W E M Smith	1958-1964
P F Courtney	1945-1947	J A Temple	1958-1962
P C Phillips *SLESS 1944-*	1945-1972		& 1964
Mrs C Kennard	1946-1983	M D Prichard	1958
C A Rust	1947	C J A Curtis	1959-1964
P D Owen	1947	M E Denning	1959-1968
P H W Salt	1947	A Ford	1959
W J McCloy	1947-1980	D W Johnson	1959-1994
H O Cooper	1947-1949	J G Adams	1959-1964
R R S Barker	1947-1977	E C Francis	1960-1961
G R Harnley	1947-1958	R A Hutchings	1960-1964
T C Ratcliffe	1947-1948	T L Macartney	1960-1981
- Churchill	1947	- Pritchard	1960
W J O'Hara	1947-1978	M H Rosenburg	1960-1961
K A Spring AOB	1948-1966	A J Bowen AOB	1961-1967
W M S Boyd	1948-1961	C Brock	1961-1962
A E Clarke	1948-1961	J S Clarke	1961-1993
A J B Spaull	1948	D Clayre	1961-1966
F H Kennard AOB	1948-1974	G L Cooksey	1961-1964
W R Rushworth AOB	1948-1954	B Crossley	1961-1962
G D McDonald	1949-1955	W M S Jamison	1961-1966
J F Chambers	1949-1954	N P T Osmer	1961-1966
T Gascoigne	1949-1973	D M W Bolton	1962-1963
A Ecclestone	1949-1957	D R Hawkey	1962-1965
J W Henry	1949-1957	C R Higgs	1962-1967
G H E Holley	1949-1955	S C Marians AOB	1962
J M Croft	1950-1955	J A R Rice AOB	1962-1967
K J Grace AOB	1949-1958	D R Rutnam AOB	1962-1968
W F Castle	1953-1959	M N E Symonds	1962-1963
J G Rogers	1954-1959	P A Badmin AOB	1963-1964

P E Kingman	1963-	C Page	1969-1985
G R McMillan	1963-1985	R W Pattullo	1969-1975
R P Mayho	1963-1965	J R L Swain	1969-1973
C T Robertson	1963-1969	J E Brand	1970-1974
D J Bunker	1964-1967	I P Davies	1970-1992
J A F Burns	1964-1972	P J V Coy	1970-1973
D B Henderson	1964-1965	R J S Skelly	1970-
C W Mathews	1964-1966	D T M Daniells	1970-1973
A W Mathias	1964-1968	E R France	1970-1973
D W Midgley	1964-1993	R E Triggs	1970-1972
R K Thomas	1964-1966	H N Cleeve	1971-1974
T Hodgkiss	1965-1990	T R Jones	1971-1972
K D Jones	1965-1970	C L Liffen	1971-
G R Mason	1965-1968	Mrs M Major	1971-1973
J W U Roberts	1965-1969	R G Miller	1971-1982
C A Rouse	1965-1993	Revd B Stowe	1971-1975
J L Beswetherick	1966-1972	D S Welham	1971-1974
A T Davies	1966-1967	J C Buckman	1972-1983
M C Grassley	1966-1973	R Hodgson	1972-1973
G Howard	1966-1971	E M D Jones	1972-
P M Lawrence	1956	N W Lee	1972-1976
	& 1966-1968	P March	1972-1974
E Marsh	1966-1972	B J Monckton	1972-1973
R F Williams	1966-1971	I Sandbrook	1972-1973
K R W Blunt	1967-1971	G Bradbury	1972-1973
Miss S M Brizzell	1967-1968	D P Stretton	1972-
J Durham	1967-1968	T W Tindale	1972-1978
D S Eastes	1967-1969	D A Vaughan	1972-1977
A E Evans	1967-1972	D E Wallis	1972-
J J Harding	1967-1975	A G Berry	1973-1996
R A Vigurs	1967-1972	J J Walsh	1973-1974
H V Wale	1967-1979	C E Bowyer	1973-1974
M J Hudson	1968	J A Brew	1973-1987
D G Brook	1968-1972	G Care	1973-1980
D H Cobb	1968-1973	F H L Chow	1973-
R J Essam	1968-1971	G E Clements AOB	1973-1975
P Major	1968-1972	P L Friedlander	1973-
F P G Musson	1968-1969	C Marvin	1973-1987
M J Quinn	1968-1969	G Massey	1973-1975
M E Shepherd	1968-1978	B M Rothbart	1973-1979
C P Williams AOB	1968-1969	Miss R de Souza	1973-1975
G J Beck	1969-1973	J Vickers AOB	1973
R W Brett	1969-1970	D Wood	1975
A C Darkins	1969-1970	B Allsopp	1974-1977
R Gallop	1969-1974	G Bayley	1974-1976
G J Haigh	1969-1970	G Caldbeck	1974-1980
J Jaworski	1969-1972	Mrs P T Cox	1974-1987
J W Newton	1969-1988	P Chirgwin	1974

P R C Wood	1974-1975	Mrs R Jones (née Sutton)	1979-1984
P J Barlow	1974-	Mrs I Termanis	1979-
A King	1974-1987	Miss M J Walker	1979-
J G Lilly	1974-	M J Walsh	1979-1991
M P Lempriere	1974-1979	D A Weale	1979-1981
P R Sherlock	1974-	T M Cunniffe	1980-1984
Mrs O G Lord (née Lynch)	1974-1979	Mrs J K Bowen-Jones	1980-
Mrs P A Barden	1975-1985	Mrs G Edwards	1980-1997
N H F Copestick	1975-1976	Miss J E Elliott	1980-1984
A W Brown	1975-1976	S A C Gorard	1980-1991
T E Davies	1975-1976	Mrs H B Johnson	1980-1984
R W Eglese	1975-1978	B K McCabe	1980-1991
J S Fairhurst	1975-1980	Mrs J Sanjana	1980-1984
P F Smith	1975-	D J Spedding	1980-1987
Mrs E M Wright	1975-	A C Warren	1980-1997
Mrs J M Alder	1976-1985	M R Blake	1981-1991
Mrs G L Butler	1976-1997	Mrs J M Constantine	1981-1985
(Lady Butler of Brockwell)		(née Leith)	
C D Chivers	1976-1982	Mrs M G Oliver	1981-1983
C Geller	1976-1977	Revd R M D Oram	1981-1987
Miss S J Frost	1976-1978	Miss P S Price	1981-1983
Mrs G M Grimwood	1976-1979	P D Meaden	1982-1996
Revd P W D Ind	1976-1981	L Mannings	1982-1989
C P Stokes	1976-1981	S E H Marker	1982-
Mrs A I Timberlake	1976-1978	Mrs C J M Nash	1982-1988
Mrs E A Akhurst	1977-1978	(née Peterson)	
T J Bell	1977-1980	J Shepherd	1982-1993
J F C Nash	1977-1998	A M Stodolny	1982-1983
C W Radice	1977-1979	Mrs K Crabtree	1983-1985
Mrs M C Rolfe	1977-1986	B D Boothroyd	1983-1984
Miss A R Chapman	1978-1982	A M Bruni	1983-
Mrs A Grey-Davies	1978-1979	P Crisan	1983-1993
Miss S A Lane	1978-	Mrs M Edwards	1983
Mrs V Madden	1978-1979	Mrs J E D Skinner	1983
M J Salmon	1978-1994	N R Fellows	1983-1986
A York``	1978-	M C Morrish	1983-1995
Mrs J Cary-Elwes	1979	D L Rosen	1983-1986
C Frostick	1979	Mrs J A Turner	1983-1987
P D Alder	1979-1980	Mrs G M Grimwood	1983
Mrs A J Elliott	1979-1983	Mrs L M Matley	1983-1986
(née Atkins)		H Clarke	1984-
C W Carden	1979-1984	D M Usborne	1984-
M Fosten	1979-	Mrs J Considine	1984
G D Ironside	1979-1983	S E Smith	1984-
Mrs E Chivers	1979-1995	Miss K E Fyfe	1984-1985
(née McGann)		Mrs R G Offergelt	1984-1986
Mrs J A Robertson	1979-1986	Mrs P M B Garbutt	1984-1990
	& 1991-	Miss W L Collins	1984-

Miss S J Dobson	1984-1985	J Ewing	1989
Mrs J James (née Hudson)	1985-1990	Dr J M Warwick	1990-1997
Miss L A Dolata	1985-1990	(Mrs Salmon)	
T G E Pennant	1985-1990	S J Collison	1990-1995
Miss J Taylor	1985-1994	J N C Walton	1990-
Miss H E Brooks	1985-1987	G McLanachan	1990-1997
G D Jenkins	1985-1995	T J R Walsh	1990-
R J P Lowry	1985-1988	Miss S P Chandler	1990-
G Reid	1985-	Miss A Hamburger	1990-
Miss D J Craven	1985-1998	Mrs A Zander	1990-
Mme M D A Ganter	1986-1990	Dr V Davis	1990-1992
Miss C M Periton	1986	Mrs B Portwin	1991-
Mrs D Denton	1986-1987	G Helliwell	1991-1995
Mrs J A Harris	1986-1987	R G Halladay	1991-
Mrs M J Skyrme	1986-1997	M S Grant	1991-
Mrs G M Lowen	1986-1994	Miss L Dunn	1991-1994
Mrs C J Clifford	1986-1988	C Lynn	1991-1993
(née Griffiths)		Miss M Brady	1991-1994
Miss J M Debenham	1986-	Mrs J Stout	1991-1997
Mrs J L Ash	1986-1992	Mrs E D French	1991-
Mrs M Hill	1986-1997	D P Williams	1992-
R B Coyle	1986-1987	Miss C L Bracken	1992-
Miss D M Whitham	1986-1987	Revd S C Dalwood	1992-
Mrs S M Davies	1987-	Miss N Pryse	1992-1994
P Thomas	1987-1997	P Boddington	1992-1996
Mrs J M Helm	1987-	Miss A Bailey	1993-1996
D Fenwick	1987-1993	P M Cochrane	1993-
Miss C Eales-White	1987	Miss M Guest	1993-1996
E R Hammond	1987-	T M Mulryne	1993-
Mrs V L Chandler, *Librarian*	1987-1996	D J Tickner	1993-
Miss E L Kemp	1987-1990	Mrs R A Thomson	1993-
Mrs S Connolly	1987-	(née Swainston)	
Mrs G Burtenshaw	1987-	Z A Rogalski	1993-
Mrs A Farrow	1987	Miss R Walter	1993-1995
P C Thompson	1988-	T McCaffrey	1994-1996
R J D Sutton	1988-	C McCay	1994-1996
Miss K M Lonsdale	1988-1997	G Connors	1994
G J Tonkin	1988-	J Abrok	1994-1996
Miss F Knight	1988-1991	K C Beckley	1994-
N R Kinnear, AOB	1988-	R Anderson	1994-1995
Miss A M Pitkethly	1988-1990	P Duran	1994-1998
P J Warren	1988-1993	L Ansell	1994-
M McCaffrey	1989-	Miss N NicSheain	1994-
Miss J Whitwell	1989-1991	Mrs L Walters	1994
Mrs K L Simonds	1989-1992	Miss S Whymark	1994-1996
Mrs C M Godwin	1989-1998	Miss L Gardner	1994-
Revd J H Jones	1989-	Miss K Vinson	1994
Miss J Laws	1989-1990	Mrs S Arthur	1995-

Miss A L Boltsa	1995-	P Jewell	1997-
Mrs J L Cargill	1995-1998	A T Kermode	1997-
Miss J Mackenzie	1995-	K J Kilmartin	1997-
P A Smith	1995-	J R Skidmore	1997-
C J Arch	1996-	Miss M Smith	1997-
K D Buckland	1996-1998	A Sood-Smith	1997-
Miss N L Cowan	1996-	Miss E T Spooner	1997-
Miss L J Gabitass	1996-	Miss C H Symes	1997-
R L Geldeard	1996-	Mrs F E Twinn	1997-
J Hodgkinson	1996-	Miss C Alexander	1998-
Dr H Langelueddecke	1996-1998	Miss S Clark	1998-
J A F Lofthouse	1996-	Mrs P Hall	1998-
N J Mann	1996-1998	Mrs D Jewell	1998-
Miss A Pascual-Rodriguez	1996-	T McNeal	1998-
Miss C Purvis	1996-	R Ody	1998-
Miss N Rainger	1996-1998	Mrs S Patterson	1998-
Miss M D Knowles, *Librarian*	1996-	Miss S Ward	1998-

ALLEYN'S JUNIOR SCHOOL

HEADMISTRESSES

1992-
Mrs B M Weir

DEPUTY HEADS

Mrs J Strong	1992-1998
Miss K Mitchell	1998-

JUNIOR SCHOOL STAFF LIST

Miss S Barton	1992-1996
Ms J Brooke	1992-
P T Das Gupta	1992-
Miss J M Mills	1992-1995
Mrs J Perks	1992-
Mrs S Robinson	1992-
Mrs P J Thompson	1992-
Miss J Wakeham	1992-1994
R Westmacott	1992-1993
Miss R Barnes	1993-1998
N Townsend	1993-
Mrs E Hill	1994-1995
Mrs K Way (née Jones)	1994-1998
Miss S Harman	1995-1997
Miss W Tyler	1995-
Miss K Foley, AOG	1996-
Mme M Fortier	1997-
K J Whiskerd	1997-
Mrs S Heyworth	1998-
Mrs C S Mullis	1998-

SCHOOL CAPTAINS

1907		H E Cocksedge
1903		T J R Alexander
1904		S E Brading
1905		F L Clark
1906		B A Finn
1907		A Geale (R)
1908		S C Seymour (B)
1910		L F Masters (R)
1911		G Paterson (R)
1912		C S Herridge (C)
1913		R W West (C)
1914		J E Appleyard (Bn)
1915		H H Farthing (Tu)
1916		G B King (Bn)
1917	(Sep)	G M Brand (R)
	(Nov)	H P J Clark (S)
1918		L E Room (B)
1919		M S Shapcott (S)
1920		W C d'Leny (S)
1921		A B Clifford (R)
1922		S G N Cabeldu (S)
1923		W S Arnold (S)
1924		A P Dearsley (C)
1925		H K Prout (Bn)
1926		H C Franklin (Bn)
1927		J G F Dee (S)
1928		C E Curtis (Ty)
1929		E Sayle (R)
1930		E H Gilmour (D)
1931		J Laughlin (Ty)
1932		F H Malpress (R)
1933		A T Parsons (C)
1934		B G H Rowley (C)
1935		C S Pickard (Bn)
1936		L A M Brannan(C)
1937		N B Balaam (D)
1938		B C R Smith (S)
1939		P R Noakes (C)
1940		B C R Parker (S)
1941	(Jan)	D G Bickford-Smith (C)
	(Mar)	J.E. Silvester (D)
1941	(Sep)	S H Giles (Bn)
1942		P Philpot (B)
1941	(Apr)	J W Macanuff (Tu)

	(Sep)	T H Land (S)
1944	(Jan)	B J Wilson (R)
	(Oct)	L Cranfield (C)
1945	(Apr)	R L J Ferne (Tu)
	(Sep)	R A Nash (Tu)
1946		T D O Lewis (Tu)
1947	(Jan)	A C Bate (Tu)
	(Sep)	L F Walker (Bn)
1949	(Jan)	R Birmingham (S)
1950	(Jan)	J F Maple (Bn)
	(Sep)	B R Higgins (D)
1951	(Jan)	R T Foster (B)
	(Sep)	G Garrett (Bn)
1951		P J Stokeley (D)
1954		J M Wales (R)
1955		C S Cook (R)
1956		R S H Brunt (Ty)
1957		E A Green (B)
1958	(Jan)	B K Andrews (R)
	(Sep)	M J Edwards (S)
1959		R W C Crickwood (R)
1960		S A F Ward (R)
1961		M J Smith (B)
1962		D J Thomas (Tu)
1963		R L Dolby (C)
1964	(May)	J Owen (Bn)
	(Sep)	B W Langley (R)
1965		A G Leech (R)
1966		E R Ayling (Bn)
1967		B Ware-Lane (R)
1968		M J Griffiths (Ty)
1969		S J Drywood (B)
1970		B R Thomson (D)
1971		J A Reynolds (C)
1972		S C Brassell (B)
1973		C C Quinlan (Tu)
1974	(Apr)	J R Mason (Ty)
	(Sep)	C H Langton (Bn)
1975		C Burgess (Tu)
1976		D C H S Vaughan (D)
1977		A V Juggins (R)
1978	(Jan)	A T Hanton (R)
	(Nov)	C P Quirk (C)
1979		C M Grant (Ty)

1980	(Sep)	P C Driscoll (B)	1990	Ali Kadifachi (Ty)
	(Nov)	N A Andrews (Ty)	1991	Hilary Strong (S)
1981		A K Kakkar (R)	1992	Anya Serota (C)
1982		Katherine McQuail (C)	1993	Vicky Shepherd (B)
1983		Reno Antoniades (Tu)	1994	Ben Woodd (Ty)
1984		Peter Last (B)	1995	Celia Bygrave (B)
1985		Madeleine Higgins (D)	1996	Peter Jenkins (R)
1986		Penny Morley (R)	1997	Claire Tovar (Bn)
1987		Natasha Miller (Tu)	1998	Rachel Reynolds (Ty)
1988		Damon Guirdham (Tu)	1999	
1989		Leilah Dare (Bn)	2000	

Michael Llewellyn-Smith,
School Captain 1961–62
Town Clerk of Adelaide, Australia

"It has taken 100 years for a girl to be
appointed School Captain. It would not
surprise me if it took a second hundred
years before we have a woman as Head
and perhaps a third before we have one
as Archbishop of York"
Katherine McQuail

COMBINED CADET FORCE
formerly Junior Training Corps and Officers' Training Corps

COMMANDING OFFICERS

Major H Gregory	1923-1928
Captain A Spring	1928-1932
Major E C Eayrs	1932-1936
Major S R Hudson	1936-1945
Major J A Taylor, T.D.	1945-1949
Lt. Col. L A R Shackleton, T.D.	1949-1960
Major K A Spring, T.D.	1960-1966
Lt. Col. J Logan	1966-1968
Major T E Evans	1968-1975
Lt. Col. A S Jenkins, T.D	1975-1982
Commander T Hodgkiss	1982-1989
Lt. Col. E M D Jones	1990-

SENIOR WARRANT OFFICERS Since 1980

Jeffrey Blyth	1980
Neil Barber	1981
Richard Giffin	1982
Patrick Utting	1983
Elizabeth Chandler	1984
Richard Godin	1985
Mark Stroud	1986
Anthony Fahey	1987
Saul Henry	1988
Timothy White	1989
Matthew Humber	1990
Andrew Strong	1991
Angharad Walters*	1992
Louise Maliphant	1993
Joanna Wozniak*	1994
David Montenegro and Ben Woodd*	1995
Michael Laws	1996
Peter Mitchener	1997
Rhian Deakin	1998

Army unless marked with an asterisk indicating RAF

BIBLIOGRAPHY

Manuscript Sources

At Alleyn's School 1914–1922	A Castle
Housemasters in the 1920s	J.B. Field
Information on the Old Boys' Club	W S Arnold
Prefects' Record Book	
School and other notebooks	K. Harvey Packer
The School 1932–1982	A.S. Jenkins
Schoolmaster in the Henderson Era	R.H.D. Young
Short History of Alleyn's School 1606–1918	J.A.R. Rice
Memories of Alleyn's	Brien O'Brien
The Memories of	G.E.J. Swift
	H.W.P. Harrison
	P.J. Reeve
	P.C. Rodway

Privately issued

Dulwich Millennium Pageant	devised by A.R. Chandler
375 Anniversary Pageant	A.R. Chandler & A.D. Rossetti

Published Sources

Alleyn's – The First Century	A.R. Chandler
Christ's Chapel of Alleyn's College of God's Gift 1990	A.R. Chandler
Christ's Chapel of Alleyn's College of God's Gift 1970	Chandler, Perry and Others
Dulwich History and Romance	E.T. Hall
Dulwich Village	D.H. Allport
Edward Alleyn Magazine 1890 onwards	
History of Camberwell	W.H. Blanch
School Magazine 1901–1904	
Scriblerus 1969–1997	
Survey of London, Vol. XXII Bankside	London County Council
350th Anniversary of the Foundation	D. Banwell
375th Anniversary of the Foundation	A.R. Chandler

INDEX

189

191